TO THE READER

Dianetics (from Greek *dia* "through," and *nous* "soul") delineates fundamental principles of the mind and spirit. Through the application of these discoveries, it became apparent that Dianetics dealt with a beingness that defied time—the human spirit—originally denominated the "I" and subsequently the "thetan." From there, Mr. Hubbard continued his research, eventually mapping the path to full spiritual freedom for the individual.

Dianetics is a forerunner and substudy of Scientology which, as practiced by the Church, addresses only the "thetan" (spirit), which is senior to the body, and its relationship to and effects on the body.

This book is presented in its original form and is part of L. Ron Hubbard's religious literature and works and is not a statement of claims made by the author, publisher or any Church of Scientology. It is a record of Mr. Hubbard's observations and research into life and the nature of man.

Neither Dianetics nor Scientology is offered as, nor professes to be physical healing, nor is any claim made to that effect. The Church does not accept individuals who desire treatment of physical or mental illness but, instead, requires a competent medical examination for physical conditions, by qualified specialists, before addressing their spiritual cause.

The Hubbard® Electrometer, or E-Meter, is a religious artifact used in the Church. The E-Meter, by itself, does nothing and is only used by ministers and ministers-in-training, qualified in its use, to help parishioners locate the source of spiritual travail.

The attainment of the benefits and goals of Dianetics and Scientology requires each individual's dedicated participation, as only through one's own efforts can they be achieved.

We hope reading this book is the first step of a personal voyage of discovery into this new and vital world religion.

THIS BOOK BELONGS TO

_____

SELF ANALYSIS

Enjoy
Leicester
Libraries

Leicester
City Council

Book due for return by last date shown.
If not reserved by another user it may be renewed.
24/7 – Renewals, Reservations, Catalogue
www.leicester.gov.uk/libraries
Book Renewal Line: (0116) 299 5430
Charges may be payable on overdue items

SELF ANALYSIS

A SIMPLE SELF-HELP VOLUME OF TESTS AND PROCESSES
BASED ON THE DISCOVERIES CONTAINED IN DIANETICS

L. RON HUBBARD

new·era®
Publications International ApS

A
HUBBARD®
Publication

NEW ERA® PUBLICATIONS
INTERNATIONAL ApS
Store Kongensgade 53
1264 Copenhagen K, Denmark

ISBN 87-7989-745-2

IMPORTANT NOTE

In reading this book, be very certain you never go past a word you do not fully understand. The only reason a person gives up a study or becomes confused or unable to learn is because he or she has gone past a word that was not understood.

The confusion or inability to grasp or learn comes AFTER a word the person did not have defined and understood. It may not only be the new and unusual words you have to look up. Some commonly used words can often be misdefined and so cause confusion.

This datum about not going past an undefined word is the most important fact in the whole subject of study. Every subject you have taken up and abandoned had its words which you failed to get defined.

Therefore, in studying this book be very, very certain you never go past a word you do not fully understand. If the material becomes confusing or you can't seem to grasp it, there will be a word just earlier that you have not understood. Don't go any further, but go back to BEFORE you got into trouble, find the misunderstood word and get it defined.

GLOSSARY

To aid reader comprehension, L. Ron Hubbard directed the editors to provide a glossary. This is included in the Appendix, *Editor's Glossary of Words, Terms and Phrases.* Words sometimes have several meanings. The *Editor's Glossary* only contains the definitions of words as they are used in this text. Other definitions can be found in standard language or Dianetics and Scientology dictionaries.

If you find any other words you do not know, look them up in a good dictionary.

CONTENTS

---

*To those hundreds of thousands of ardent Dianetics supporters
who have carried the guidon of sanity against
the crumbling citadels of Superstition and who have
succeeded in rallying to their standard the hopes of Man.*

D O NOT HARKEN TOO WELL TO HE WHO WOULD TELL YOU THIS SYSTEM WILL NOT WORK. HE WOULD NOT FEEL SAFE IF PEOPLE AROUND HIM GREW TOO STRONG. THE WISE MAN TESTS BEFORE HE TALKS. THE CRITIC BUT FOLLOWS THE FAD OF A CYNICAL AND APATHETIC AGE. YOU HAVE A RIGHT TO YOUR OWN OPINION. THIS SYSTEM WORKS OR IT DOESN'T ACCORDING TO YOUR EXPERIENCE. NOT ALL THE AUTHORITIES IN CHRISTENDOM CAN ALTER NATURAL LAW.

INTRODUCTION

S*elf Analysis* cannot revive the dead.

Self Analysis will not empty insane asylums or stop war. These are the tasks of the Dianetic auditor and the Group Dianetic technician.

But *Self Analysis* will conduct you on the most interesting adventure in your life. The adventure of *you*.

How efficient are you? What are your potentials? How much can you improve? Well, basically your intentions toward yourself and your fellow man are *good*. Basically, if sometimes clouded over with the not-so-pale cast of bad experience, your potentialities are a great deal better than anyone ever permitted you to believe.

Take your memory, a small part of your total assets. Is it perfect? Can you, at will, recall everything you have ever learned or heard, every phone number, every name? If you can't, you can see that there is room for improvement. Now somebody, with a half glance at the title page of this book, will try to assume that *Self Analysis* simply improves memory. That is like saying that all a train can do is meet schedules. It does much more.

But memory is a starter. If your memory were as accurate as a computer and even faster, you would be more efficient and more comfortable and it would certainly save writing those notes you have to make. Yes, you probably couldn't have *too* good a memory on things you've studied and things you need.

But there are a lot of things as important as memory. There's your reaction time. Most people react too slowly in emergencies. Let's say it takes you half a second to pull your hand off a hot stove. That's many times too long a period to have your hand on that stove.

Or let's say you require a third of a second to see the car ahead stop and to start to put on your own brakes. That's too long. A lot of accidents happen because of slow reaction time.

In the case of an athlete, reaction time is a direct index as to how capable he may be in a sport. So it assists one in many ways to be able to react quickly.

Self Analysis speeds up reaction time. Here's a trick. Take a dollar bill, unfolded. Have somebody hold it vertically above your hand. Open your thumb and index finger just below the lower edge of the bill. Now let your friend let go. You try to close thumb and index finger on the bill. Did you miss it, snapping after it had gone all the way through? That's very slow reaction. Did you catch it by its upper edge when it was almost gone? That's much too slow. Did you catch it on Washington's face? That's fair. Or did you catch it on the lower edge, even before it really got started? That's the way it should be. Fewer accidents, greater general alertness. Well, barring actual physical damage to hand or arm, *Self Analysis* will speed that up for you.

Do you have trouble going to sleep or getting up? Do you feel a little tired a lot of the time? Well, that can be remedied.

As for what they call psychosomatic illnesses—sinusitis, allergies, some heart trouble, "bizarre" aches and pains, poor eyesight, arthritis, etc., etc., etc., down through 70 percent of Man's ills—*Self Analysis* should be able to help markedly.

Then there's the matter of how young or old you may look. *Self Analysis* can make quite a change there.

And there's the matter of plain ordinary ability to be happy in life and enjoy things. And there *Self Analysis* shines brightly. For it can raise your tone fast enough, usually, so that even you will agree things can be good.

As my boyhood hero, Charles Russell, the painter, once described a certain potion, "It'd make a jack rabbit spit in a wolf's eye." Now maybe *Self Analysis* doesn't always have this effect, but it happens regularly enough to be usual. Certain it is that the user often goes through such a period, much to the alarm of his friends. *Self Analysis* does have an effect as in the song:

"I can lick that guy, I can kiss that girl,

"I can ride that bronc and make him whirl..."

The moral and caution is, "Don't pick too big a wolf." At least not until you've been using this for a while and kind of get things in proportion again.

In short, this is an adventure. How good can you get?

A lot depends on how good you are potentially—but you can be assured that that's a lot better than you ever supposed. And it's a cinch it's better than your friends would ever tell you.

Please don't be discouraged if you find yourself pretty low on the self-evaluation chart later on. All is not lost. The Processing Section can boost you up at a good rate if you keep at it.

And don't be surprised if you suddenly begin to feel uncomfortable while you're working on the Processing Section. You can expect that to happen every now and then. Just keep going. If it gets too bad, simply turn to the last section and answer those questions a few times and you should start feeling better very soon.

All I'm trying to tell you is this—adventures are dull if a little excitement doesn't crop up. And you can expect excitement—too much in some places.

You are going to know a lot about you when you finally finish.

All this is on your own responsibility. Anything as powerful as these processes can occasionally flare. If you are fairly stable mentally, there is no real danger. But I will not mislead you. A man could go mad simply reading this book. If you see somebody who isn't quite as stable as he thinks he is working with *Self Analysis,* coax it away from him. If he can barely stand mental chicken broth, he has no right to be dining on raw meat. Send him to see a Dianetic auditor. And even if he does throw a wheel, a Dianetic auditor can straighten him out. Just send for an auditor.

Don't, then, disabuse yourself of the fact that *Self Analysis* can send the unstable spinning.

We're dealing here with the root stuff of why men go mad. If it isn't explained in the text, it will be found in a standard work on Dianetics. Even so, it is doubtful if *Self Analysis* could create as much madness in a year as an income tax blank from our thorough, if somewhat knuckleheaded, government.

Now to particulars. You'll find the tests in Chapter Eight. You can take the first one. It will give you a figure which will place you on the chart. Don't blame me if it's a low score. Blame your parents or the truant officer.

Next, it would probably interest you to read the text. It will give you a different viewpoint on things, possibly. It is regretted if it is too simple for the savant or too complex or something. It's simply an effort to write in American a few concepts about the mind based on a lot of technical material in Dianetics, but made more palatable. You'll do better on the processing if you read the text.

The Processing Section, Chapter Ten, has a large number of parts. You can simply work straight through or work over each one again and again, until you feel you've sufficiently explored that part of your life. In any case, you will go through every section many times.

To help you there is a two-sided disk in the back of the book.

Thus you are prepared to go exploring into your own life. That's an interesting adventure for anyone. I've done what I could to make it easier. Don't be too harsh on me, however, if you get grounded up some long-lost river and eaten by cannibals or engrams. The last section will help get you out. What's left of you, anyway.

Don't get fainthearted and slack off, though, when you find the going rough. It's easy to quit. And then you'd never know just what you really are, basically.

Going to take the whole trip? You're a brave person. I compliment you.

May you never be the same again.

L. RON HUBBARD

CHAPTER ONE

ON GETTING TO
KNOW OURSELVES

ON GETTING TO KNOW OURSELVES

A re you a friend of yours?

Probably the most neglected friend you have is you. And yet every man, before he can be a true friend to the world, must first become a friend to himself.

In this society, where aberration flourishes in the crowded cities and marts of business, few are the men who have not been subjected, on every hand, to a campaign to convince them that they are much less than they think they are.

You would fight anyone who said of your friends what is implied about you. It is time you fought for the best friend you will ever have—yourself.

The first move in striking up this friendship is to make an acquaintance with what you are and what you might become. "Know thyself!" said the ancient Greek. Until recently it was not possible to make a very wide acquaintance. Little was known about human behavior as a science. But atomic physics, in revealing new knowledge to Man, has also revealed the general characteristics of the energy of life. And by that, a great deal can be known which was not before suspected.

You do not need to know atomic physics to know yourself, but you need to know something of the apparent goal of life in general and your own goals in particular.

In a later chapter there are some questions you can answer which will give you a better insight into your capabilities as they are and what they can become—and do not be deceived, for they can become a great deal more than you ever before suspected.

Just now let's talk about the general goal of all life. From whence did we come and whither are we going? Knowing that, we can know something about the basic laws which motivate your own urges and behavior.

All problems are basically simple—once you know the fundamental answer. And this is no exception in life. For thousands of years men strove to discover the underlying drives of existence. And in an enlightened age, when exploration of the universes had already yielded enough secrets to give us A-bombs, it became possible to explore for and find the fundamental law of life. What would you do if you had this fundamental law? How easily, then, would you understand all the puzzles, riddles and complexities of personality and behavior? You could understand conjurers and bank presidents, colonels and coolies, kings, cats and coal heavers. And more important, you could easily predict what they would do in any given circumstance and you would know what to expect from anyone without any guesswork—indeed with a security diabolical in its accuracy.

"In the beginning was the Word," but what was the Word? What fundamental principle did it outline? What understanding would one have if he knew it?

An ancient Persian king once made a great effort to know this Word. He tried to discover it by having his sages boil down all the knowledge of the world.

At his orders, every book written which could be obtained was collected together in an enormous library. Books were brought to that ancient city by the caravanload. And the wise men of the time worked for years condensing every piece of knowledge which was known into a single volume.

But the king wanted a better statement of the fundamental Word. And he made his sages reduce that volume to a single page. And he made them reduce it again to a sentence. And then, after many more years of study, his philosophers finally obtained that single Word, the formula which would solve all riddles.

And the city died in war and the Word was lost.

But what was it? Certainly its value, since it would make an understanding of Man possible, exceeded the riches of Persia. Two thousand years later, out of the studies of atomic and molecular phenomena, we can again postulate what that Word was. And use it. Use it to know ourselves. And to predict the actions of other men.

ON THE LAWS OF SURVIVAL AND ABUNDANCE

ON THE LAWS OF SURVIVAL AND ABUNDANCE

The Dynamic Principle of Existence is: SURVIVAL!

At first glance that may seem too basic. It may seem too simple. But when we examine this word, we find some things about it which make it possible for us to do tricks with it. And to know things which were never known before.

Knowledge could be represented by a pyramid. At the top we would have a simple fact, but a fact so widely embracing the universe that many facts could be known from it. From this point we could conceive descending down into greater and greater numbers of facts, represented by the broadening of the pyramid.

At any point we examine this pyramid we would find that as one descended, he would find facts of wider and less-related meanings. As one went up, he would find greater and greater simplicities. Science is the process of starting low on the pyramid, much like the Persian king, and rising up in an effort to discover more basic facts which explain later facts. Philosophy could be said to be the operation of taking very basic facts and then leading them into explanations of greater and greater numbers of facts.

At the point of our pyramid, we have SURVIVAL!

It is as though, at some remarkably distant time, the Supreme Being gave forth a command to all life: "Survive!" It was not said how to survive nor yet how long. All that was said was "Survive!" The reverse of "Survive!" is "Succumb." And that is the penalty for not engaging in survival activities.

But what of such things as morals, ideals, love? Don't these things go above "mere survival"? Unfortunately or fortunately, they do not.

When one thinks of survival, one is apt to make the error of thinking in terms of "barest necessity." That is not survival. For it has no margin for loss.

The engineer, when he constructs a bridge, uses something called a "factor of safety." If a bridge is to hold ten tons, he builds it to hold fifty tons. He makes that bridge five times as strong. Then he has a margin for deterioration of materials, overloading, sudden and unforeseen stress of elements, and any accident which may occur.

In life, the only real guarantee of survival is *abundance*.

A farmer who calculates to need twelve bushels of grain for his food for a year and plants twelve bushels has cut back his chances of survival very markedly. The fact is, he will not survive unless some neighbor has been more prudent. For the grasshoppers will take part of the wheat. And the drought will take some. And the hail will take some. And the tax gatherer will take some. And what will he do for seed wheat if he intends to use all he plants for food?

No, the farmer who knows he has to eat twelve bushels of wheat in the coming year had better plant a hundred. Then the grasshoppers and Internal Revenue people can chew away as they will. The farmer will still be able to harvest enough for his own food except, of course, in a socialism—where nobody survives, at least for very long!

An individual survives or succumbs in ratio to his ability to acquire and hold the wherewithal of survival. The security of a good job, for instance, means some guarantee of survival—other threats to existence not becoming too overpowering. The man who makes a good living can afford better clothing against the weather, a sounder and better home, medical care for himself and his family, good transportation and, what is important, the respect of his fellows. All these things are survival.

Of course, the man who makes a good living can have such a worrisome job, can excite so much envy from his fellows and can be so harassed that he loses something of his survival potential. But even a subversive will change his political coat if you offer him enough money.

Take the man who makes barely a living wage. He wears clothes which protect him very poorly. Thus he can easily become ill. He lives in a place which but ill defends him from the weather. He is haggard with concern. For his level of survival is so low that he has no margin, no abundance. He cannot bank anything against the day he becomes ill. And he cannot pay a doctor. And he can take no vacations. Even in a collective state, his lot would be such, his regimentation so thorough that he could do little to protect his own survival.

Youth has a survival abundance over old age, for youth still has endurance. And the dreams of youth—good survival stuff, dreams—are not yet broken by failures. Youth has, in addition, a long expectancy. And that is important, for survival includes length of time to live.

As for ideals, as for honesty, as for one's love of one's fellow man, one cannot find good survival for one or for many where these things are absent. The criminal does not survive well. The average criminal spends the majority of his adult years caged like some wild beast and guarded from escape by the guns of good marksmen. A man who is known to be honest is awarded survival—good jobs, good friends. And the man who has his ideals, no matter how thoroughly the minions of the Devil may wheedle him to desert them, survives well only so long as he is true to those ideals. Have you ever heard about a doctor who, for the sake of gain, begins to secretly attend criminals or peddle dope? That doctor does not survive long after his ideals are laid aside.

In short, the most esoteric concepts fall within this understanding of SURVIVAL! One survives so long as he is true to himself, his family, his friends, the laws of the universe. When he fails in any respect, his survival is cut down.

The end of survival, however, is no sharp thing. Survival is not a matter of being alive this moment and dead the next. Survival is actually a graduated scale.

ON THE DEATH
OF CONSCIOUSNESS

ON THE DEATH
OF CONSCIOUSNESS

Where does one cease to Survive and begin to Succumb? The point of demarcation is not death as we know it. It is marked by what one might call the death of the consciousness of the individual.

Man's greatest weapon is his reason. Lacking the teeth, the armor-plate hide, the claws of so many other life forms, Man has relied upon his ability to reason in order to further himself in his survival.

The selection of the ability to think as a chief weapon is a fortunate one. It has awarded Man with the kingdom of Earth. Reason is an excellent weapon. The animal with his teeth, with his armor-plated hide, with his long claws, is fixed with weapons he cannot alter. He cannot adjust to a changing environment. And it is terribly important, to survive, to change when the environment changes. Every extinct species became extinct because it could not change to control a new environment. Reason remedies this failure to a marked extent. For Man can invent new tools and new weapons and a whole new environment. Reason permits him to change to fit new situations. Reason keeps him in control of new environments.

Any animal that simply adjusts itself to match its environment is doomed. Environments change rapidly. Animals which control and change the environment have the best chance of survival.

The only way you can organize a collective state is to convince men that they must adjust and adapt themselves, like animals, to a constant environment. The people must be deprived of the right to control, as individuals, their environment. Then they can be regimented and herded into groups. They become owned, not owners. Reason and the right to reason must be taken from them, for the very center of reason is the right to make up one's own mind about one's environment.

The elements fight Man and man fights man. The primary target of the enemies of Man or a man is his right and ability to reason. The crude and blundering forces of the elements, storms, cold and night bear down against, challenge and then mayhap crush the reason as well as the body.

But just as unconsciousness always precedes death, even by instants, so does the death of reason precede the death of the organism. And this action may happen in a long span of time, even half a lifetime, even more.

Have you watched the high alertness of a young man breasting the forces which oppose life? And watched another in old age? You will find that what has suffered has been the ability to reason. He has gained hard-won experience and on this experience he seeks, from middle age on, to travel. It is a truism that youth thinks fast on little experience. And that age thinks slowly on much. The reason of youth is very far from always right, for youth is attempting to reason without adequate data.

Suppose we had a man who had retained all his ability to reason and yet had a great deal of experience. Suppose our graybeards could think with all the enthusiasm and vitality of youth and yet had all their experience as well. Age says to youth, "You have no experience!" Youth says to age, "You have no vision, you will not accept or even examine new ideas!" Obviously an ideal arrangement would be for one to have the experience of age and the vitality and vision of youth.

You may have said to yourself, "With all my experience now, what wouldn't I give for some of the enthusiasm I had once." Or perhaps you have excused it all by saying you have "lost your illusions." But you aren't sure that they were illusions. Are brightness in life, quick enthusiasm, a desire and will to live, a belief in destiny—are these things illusions? Or are they symptoms of the very stuff of which vital life is made? And isn't their decline a symptom of death?

Knowledge does not destroy a will to live. Pain and loss of self-determinism destroy that will. Life can be painful. The gaining of experience is often painful. The retaining of that experience is essential. But isn't it still experience if it doesn't yet have the pain?

Suppose you could wipe out of your life all the pain, physical and otherwise, which you have accumulated. Would it be so terrible to have to part with a broken heart or a psychosomatic illness, with fears and anxieties and dreads?

Suppose a man had a chance again, with all he knows, to look life and the universe in the eye again and say it could be whipped.

Do you recall a day when you were younger and you woke to find bright dew sparkling on the grass, the leaves, to find the golden Sun bright upon a happy world? Do you recall how beautiful and fine it once was? The first sweet kiss? The warmth of true friendship? The intimacy of a moonlight ride?

What made it become otherwise than a brilliant world?

The consciousness of the world around one is not an absolute thing. One can be more conscious of color and brightness and joy at one time of life than another. One can more easily feel the brilliant reality of things in youth than he can in age. And isn't this something like a decline of consciousness, of awareness?

What is it that makes one less aware of the brilliance of the world around him? Has the world changed? No, for each new generation sees the glamour and the glory, the vitality of life—the same life that age may see as dull at best. The individual changes. And what makes him change? Is it a decay of his glands and sinews? Hardly, for all the work that has been done on glands and sinews—the structure of the body—has restored little if any of the brilliance of living.

"Ah, youth," sighs the adult. "If I but had your zest again!" What reduced that zest?

As one's consciousness of the brilliance of life declines, so has declined his own consciousness. Awareness decreases exactly as consciousness decreases. The ability to perceive the world around one and the ability to draw accurate conclusions about it are, to all intents, the same thing.

Glasses are a symptom of the decline of consciousness. One needs his sight bolstered to make the world look brighter. The loss of the ability to move swiftly, as one ran when he was a child, is a decline of consciousness and ability.

Complete unconsciousness is death. Half unconsciousness is half death. A quarter unconsciousness is a quarter of death. And as one accumulates the pain attendant upon life and fails to accumulate the pleasures, one gradually loses his race with the gentleman with the scythe. And there ensues, at last, the physical incapacity for seeing, thinking and being, known as death.

How does one accumulate this pain?

And if he got rid of it, would full consciousness and a full bright concept of life return?

And is there a way to get rid of it?

ON OUR EFFORTS
FOR IMMORTALITY

ON OUR EFFORTS FOR IMMORTALITY

The physical universe consists of four elements—*matter, energy, space and time.*

According to nuclear physics, matter is composed of energy such as electrons and protons. And the energy and the matter exist in space and time. All this is actually very simple. And even then we need not go very far into it to understand that the universe in which we live is composed of simple things arranged and rearranged to make many forms and manifestations.

The concrete sidewalk, the air, ice-cream sodas, paychecks, cats, kings and coal heavers are basically composed of matter, energy, space and time. And where they are alive, they contain another ingredient—*life.*

Life is an energy of a very special kind, obeying certain laws different from what we normally consider energy (such as electricity). But life is an energy and it has some peculiar properties.

Life is able to collect and organize matter and energy in space and time and animate it. Life takes some matter and energy and makes an organism such as a monocell, a tree, a polar bear or a man.

Then this organism, still animated by the energy called life, further acts upon matter and energy in space and time and further organizes and animates matter and energy into new objects and shapes.

Life could be said to be engaged upon a conquest of the physical universe. The primary urge of life has been said to be SURVIVAL! In order to accomplish survival, life has to continue and win in its conquest of the physical universe.

When life or a life form ceases to continue that conquest, it ceases to survive and succumbs.

Here we have a gigantic action. The energy of life versus matter, energy, space and time. Life versus the physical universe.

Here is an enormous struggle. The chaotic, disorganized physical universe, capable only of force, resisting the conquest of life, organizing and persistent, capable of reason.

Life learns the laws of the physical universe—matter, energy, space and time—and then turns those laws against the physical universe to further its conquest.

Man has spent much time learning what he could of the physical universe as in the sciences of physics and chemistry, but more important even, of the daily battle of life against the universe. Do not think that a monocell does not manifest a knowledge of life's working rules, for it does. What cunning it takes to organize some chemicals and sunlight into a living unit! The biologist stands in awe of the expertness of management of the smallest living cells. He gazes at these intricate and careful entities, these microscopic units of life forms, and even he cannot believe that it is all an accident.

There is life, then, a vital energy, not quite like physical universe energy. And then there are life forms.

The life form or the organism, such as a *living* human body, consists of life *plus* physical universe matter, energy, space and time. A *dead* body consists of physical universe matter, energy, space and time *minus* life energy. Life has been there, has organized and has then withdrawn from the organism, an operation we know as the cycle of conception, birth, growth, decay and death.

Although there are answers as to where life goes when it withdraws and what it then does, we need not examine that now. The important thing to a living organism is the fact that it is seeking to survive, in obedience to the whole effort of all life, and that in order to do so it must succeed in its conquest of the physical universe.

Stated simply, life must first accumulate enough matter and energy to make up an organism (such as the human body) and must then ally the organism with friendly and cooperative organisms (such as other people) and must continue to procure additional matter and energy for food, clothing and shelter in order to support itself. Additionally, in order to survive, it must do two specific things which, beyond the necessity of allies, food, clothing and shelter, are basically important.

Life must procure pleasure.

Life must avoid pain.

Life has an active thrust away from pain, which is non-survival, destructive and which is death itself. Pain is a warning of non-survival or potential death.

Life has an active thrust toward pleasure. Pleasure can be defined as the action toward obtaining or the procurement of survival. The ultimate pleasure is an infinity of survival or immortality—a goal unobtainable for the physical organism itself (but not its life), but toward which the organism strives.

Happiness, then, could be defined as the overcoming of obstacles toward a desirable goal. Any desirable goal, if closely inspected, will be found to be a survival goal.

Too much pain obstructs the organism toward survival.

Too many obstructions between the organism and survival mean non-survival.

Thus one finds the mind engaged in computing or imagining ways and means to avoid pain and reach pleasure and putting the solutions into action. And this is all that the mind does:

It perceives, poses and resolves problems relating to the survival of the organism, the future generations, the group, life and the physical universe and puts the solutions into action.

If it solves the majority of the problems presented, the organism thus achieves a high level of survival. If the organism's mind fails to resolve a majority of problems, then the organism fails.

The mind, then, has a definite relationship to survival. And one means here the whole mind, not just the brain. The brain is a structure. The mind can be considered to be the whole being, mortal and immortal, the definite personality of the organism and all its attributes.

Hence, if one's mind is working well, if it is resolving the problems it should resolve and if it is putting those solutions into proper action, the survival of the organism is well assured. If the mind is not working well, the survival of the organism is thrown into question and doubt.

One's mind, then, must be in excellent condition if he is to best guarantee the survival of himself, his family, future generations, his group and life.

The mind seeks to guarantee and direct survival actions. It seeks survival not only for the organism (self) but seeks it for the family, children, future generations and all life. Thus it can be selectively blunted. A mind can be blunted concerning the survival of self and yet be alive to the survival of future generations. It can be blunted concerning groups and yet be very alive to its responsibility for the organism (self). In order to function well, the mind must not be blunted in any direction.

To function well, the mind must conceive itself able to handle the physical universe of matter, energy, space and time within the necessities of the organism, the family, future generations and groups as well as life.

The mind must be able to avoid pain for and discover pleasure for the self, future generations, the family and the group as well as life itself.

As the mind fails to avoid pain and discover pleasure, so fails the organism, the family, future generations, the group and life.

The failure of one organism in a group to properly resolve survival problems is a failure, in part, for the whole group. Hence, "Do not send to find for whom the bell tolls, it tolls for thee!"

Life is an interdependent, cooperative effort. Each and every living organism has a part to play in the survival of other organisms.

When it comes to a thinking mind such as Man's, the organism must be able to act independently for its own survival and the survival of others. In order to accomplish these survivals, however, a mind has to be able to realize solutions which are optimum not only for self, but for all other things concerned in its survival.

Thus the mind of one organism must reach agreements with the minds of other organisms in order that all may survive to the highest possible level.

When a mind becomes dulled and blunted, it begins to compute its solutions poorly. It begins to get confused about its goals. It is not sure what it really means to do. And it will involve and inhibit the survival of other organisms. It may begin, for instance, to compute that it must survive as self and that only self is important and so neglect the survival of others. This is non-survival activity. It is highly aberrated.

A mind which begins to "survive" only for self, and begins to diminish and control with force other organisms around, is already better than halfway toward its own death. It is a mind which is less than half alive. It has less than half its actual potential. Its perception of the physical universe is poor. It does not realize that it is dependent for survival upon cooperation with others. It has lost its survival mission. This mind is already outward bound toward death, has passed its peak and will actually take personal actions which lead to its own death.

Life, the large overall life, has a use for organism death. When an organism can no longer continue well, the plan of life is to kill it and invest anew in a new organism.

Death is life's operation of disposing of an outmoded and unwanted organism so that new organisms can be born and can flourish.

Life itself does not die. Only the physical organism dies. Not even a personality, apparently, dies. Death, then, in truth, is a limited concept of the death of the physical part of the organism. Life and the personality, apparently, go on. The physical part of the organism ceases to function. And that is death.

When an organism reaches a point where it is only half conscious, where it is only perceiving half as well as it should, where it is functioning only half as well as it should, death begins. The organism, thereafter, will take actions to hasten death. It does this "unconsciously." But in its aberrated state, such a mind will also bring death to other organisms. Thus a half-conscious organism is a menace to others. Here is the accident-prone, the fascist, the person who seeks to dominate, the selfish and self-seeking person. Here is an organism outward bound.

When an organism reaches a point where it is only a third alive, a third conscious, it is perceiving only a third of what it might. Life even further hastens the death of this organism and those around it. Here is the suicide, here is the person who is continually ill, who refuses to eat.

Organisms which are outward bound toward death sometimes require years and years to die. For the organism experiences resurgences and still has some small desire to go on living. And other organisms help it to live. It is carried along by the tide of life even though its individual direction is toward death—death for others and death for self and death for the physical universe around it.

Society, the bulk of which is bent upon survival, fails or refuses to recognize death or the urge of organisms toward it. Society passes laws against murder and suicide. Society provides hospitals. Society carries such people upon its back. And society will not hear of euthanasia or "mercy killing."

Organisms which have passed the halfway point will take extraordinary measures and means to bring about death for others and for things and for self. Here we have the Hitlers, the criminals, the destructively neurotic.

Give a person who has passed this point a car to drive and the car may become involved in an accident. Give him money and the money will go to purchase non-survival things.

But we must not emphasize the dramatic and forget the important like the newspapers do. The action and urge toward death becomes noticeable only when it is very dramatic. It is most dangerous, however, in its undramatic forms.

A person who has passed the halfway point brings death to things and people on a small scale at all times. A house left dirty, appointments not kept, clothing not cared for, vicious gossip, carping criticisms of others "for their own good" –these are all enturbulences which bring failure and too many failures bring death.

And it should not be supposed that by "halfway point," one means halfway through life. It means half conscious, half alive, half (or less) perceiving and thinking. A child may be suppressed to this level by his parents and school. And, indeed, children quite ordinarily drop below the halfway point, so defeated do they become in their environment and in their contest with life. Age is no criterion. But physical health is.

The surest manifestation that someone has passed the halfway point is his physical condition. The chronically ill have passed it.

If one is to have a secure society, then, if one is to rid a society of its death factors, one must have some means of either destroying the people who bring death to it–the Hitlers, the insane, the criminals–or he must have some means of salvaging these people and bringing them back into a state of full consciousness.

Full consciousness would mean full recognition of one's responsibilities, his relationship with others, his care of himself and of society.

How can such a thing be achieved? If you could achieve it, you could raise a social order to hitherto unattainable heights. You could empty the prisons and insane asylums. You could make a world too sane for war. And people could be made well who have never had the means of it before. And people could be happy who have never truly known what happiness was. You could raise the goodwill and efficiency of all men and all social orders if you could restore the vitality of these people.

In order to know how it can be restored, one has to know how the consciousness, the vitality and the will to live become reduced.

CHAPTER FIVE

ON RAISING
OUR LEVEL OF
CONSCIOUSNESS

ON RAISING OUR LEVEL OF CONSCIOUSNESS

An organism is suppressed toward death by accumulated pain.

Pain in one great sweeping shock brings about immediate death.

Pain in small doses over a lifetime gradually suppresses the organism toward death.

What is pain?

Pain is the warning of loss. It is an automatic alarm system built into life organisms which informs the organism that some part of it or all of it is under stress and that the organism had better take action or die.

The signal of pain means that the organism is in the proximity of a destructive force or object. To ignore pain is to die. Pain is the whip which sends the organism away from hot stoves, sub-zero weather. Pain is the threat of non-survival, the punishment for errors in trying to survive.

And pain is always loss. A burned finger means that the body has lost the cells on the surface of that finger. They are dead. A blow on the head means the death of scalp and other cells in the area. The whole organism is thus warned of the proximity of a death source and so attempts to get away from it.

The loss of a loved one is also a loss of survival. The loss of a possession is also loss of survival potential. One then confuses physical pain and the loss of survival organisms or objects. And so there is such a thing as "mental pain."

But life, in its whole contest with the physical universe, has no patience with failure. An organism so foolhardy as to let itself be struck too hard and so depressed into unconsciousness stays in the vicinity of the pain-dealing object. It is considered to be non-survival if it fails so markedly to survive.

Unconsciousness experienced as a result of a blow or an illness is a quick picture of what happens over a life span.

Is there any difference, except time, between these two things?

A blow resulting in unconsciousness which results in death.

The accumulated blows over a life span resulting in a gradual lessening of consciousness resulting in eventual death.

One is slower than the other.

One of the basic discoveries of Dianetics was that unconsciousness and all the pain attendant upon it were stored in a part of the mind and that this pain and unconsciousness accumulated until they caused the organism to begin to die.

Another discovery of Dianetics was that this pain could be nullified or erased with a return to full consciousness and a rehabilitation toward survival.

In other words, with Dianetics, it became possible to cancel out the accumulated unconsciousness and pain of the years and restore the health and vitality of an organism.

Accumulated physical pain and loss bring about a reduction of consciousness, a reduction of physical health and a reduction of the will to live to a point where the organism actively, if often slyly, seeks death.

Erase or nullify the physical pain, the losses of a lifetime, and vitality returns.

The vitality of living, of seeking higher levels of survival, is life itself.

The human body was found to be extremely capable of repairing itself when the stored memories of pain were cancelled. Further, it was discovered that so long as the stored pain remained, the doctoring of what are called psychosomatic ills, such as arthritis, rheumatism, dermatitis and thousands of others, could not result in anything permanent. Psychotherapy, not knowing about pain storage and its effects, discovered long ago that one could rid a patient of one illness only to have another pop up. And psychotherapy became a defeatist school because it could do nothing permanent for the aberrated or the ill, even when it could do a little something to relieve it. Hence, *all* efforts to make men vital and well became suspect because the reason they were inefficient and ill had not been discovered and proven.

With Dianetics it became possible to eradicate aberration and illness because it became possible to nullify or eradicate the pain from the pain-storage banks of the body without applying further pain, as in surgery.

Consciousness, then, depends upon the absence or the nullification or eradication of memories of physical pain, for unconsciousness is a part of that pain—one of its symptoms.

Arthritis of the knee, for instance, is the accumulation of all knee injuries in the past. The body confuses time and environment with the time and environment where the knee was actually injured and so keeps the pain there. The fluids of the body avoid the pain area. Hence, a deposit which is called arthritis. The proof of this is that when the knee injuries of the past are located and discharged, the arthritis ceases, no other injury takes its place and the person is finished with arthritis of the knee. And this happens ten cases out of ten—except in those cases where age and physical deterioration are so well advanced toward death that the point of no return is passed.

Take a bad heart. The person has pain in his heart. He can take medicine or voodoo or another diet and still have a bad heart. Find and eradicate or nullify an actual physical injury to the heart and the heart ceases to hurt and gets well.

Nothing is easier to prove than these tenets. A good Dianetic auditor can take a broken-down, sorrow-drenched lady of thirty-eight and knock out her past periods of physical and mental pain and have on his hands somebody who appears to be twenty-five—and a bright, cheerful twenty-five at that.

Sure it's incredible. But so is an A-bomb, a few pennyweights of plutonium, which can blow a city off the chart.

Once you know the basic tenets of life and how it acts as an energy, life can be put back into the ill, the devitalized, the would-be suicide.

And more important than treating the very ill, mentally or physically, one can interrupt the downward spiral in a man who is still alert and well so that he will not thereafter become so ill. And one can take the so-called normal person and send his state of being up to levels of brilliance and success not possible before.

Restore an individual's full consciousness and you restore his full life potential.

And it can now be done.

ON RAISING OUR LEVEL OF LIFE AND BEHAVIOR

ON RAISING OUR LEVEL OF LIFE AND BEHAVIOR

The *Tone Scale*, a small edition of which is in Chapter Seven, plots the descending spiral of life from full vitality and consciousness, through half vitality and half consciousness, down to death.

By various calculations about the energy of life, by observation and by test, this Tone Scale is able to give levels of behavior as life declines.

These various levels are common to all men.

When a man is nearly dead, he can be said to be in a chronic *apathy.* And he behaves in a certain way about other things. This is 0.1 on the Tone Scale chart.

When a man is chronically in grief about his losses, he is in *grief.* And he behaves certain ways about many things. This is 0.5 on the chart.

When a person is not yet so low as grief, but realizes losses are impending or is fixed chronically at this level by past losses, he can be said to be in *fear.* This is around 1.1 on the chart.

An individual who is fighting against threatened losses is in *anger.* And he manifests other aspects of behavior. This is 1.5.

The person who is merely suspicious that loss may take place or who has become fixed at this level is resentful. He can be said to be in *antagonism*. This is 2.0 on the chart.

Above antagonism, the situation of a person is not so good that he is enthusiastic, not so bad that he is resentful. He has lost some goals and cannot immediately locate others. He is said to be in *boredom*, or at 2.5 on the Tone Scale chart.

At 3.0 on the chart, a person has a *conservative*, cautious aspect toward life, but is reaching his goals.

At 4.0 the individual is *enthusiastic*, happy and vital.

Very few people are natural 4.0s. A charitable average is probably around 2.8.

You can examine the chart and you will find in the boxes, as you go across it, the various characteristics of people at these levels. Horribly enough, these characteristics have been found to be constant. If you have a 3.0 as your rating, then you will carry across the whole chart at 3.0.

You have watched this chart in operation before now. Have you ever seen a child trying to acquire, let us say, a nickel? At first he is happy. He simply wants a nickel. If refused, he then explains why he wants it. If he fails to get it and did not want it badly, he becomes bored and goes away. But if he wants it badly, he will get antagonistic about it. Then he will become angry. Then, that failing, he may lie about why he wants it. That failing, he goes into grief. And if he is still refused, he finally sinks into apathy and says he doesn't want it. This is negation.

And you have seen the chart in reverse. A child threatened by danger also dwindles down the scale. At first he does not appreciate that the danger is posed at him and he is quite cheerful.

Then the danger, let us say it is a dog, starts to approach him. The child sees the danger, but still does not believe it is for him and keeps on with his business. But his playthings "bore" him for the moment. He is a little apprehensive and not sure. Then the dog comes nearer. The child "resents him" or shows some antagonism. The dog comes nearer still. The child becomes angry and makes some effort to injure the dog. The dog comes still nearer and is more threatening. The child becomes afraid. Fear unavailing, the child cries. If the dog still threatens him, the child may go into an apathy and simply wait to be bitten.

Objects or animals or people which assist survival, as they become inaccessible to the individual, bring him down the Tone Scale.

Objects, animals or people which threaten survival, as they approach the individual, bring him down the Tone Scale.

This scale has a chronic or an acute aspect. A person can be brought down the Tone Scale to a low level for ten minutes and then go back up. Or he can be brought down it for ten years and not go back up.

A man who has suffered too many losses, too much pain, tends to become fixed at some lower level of the scale and, with only slight fluctuations, stays there. Then his general and common behavior will be at that level of the Tone Scale.

Just as a 0.5 moment of grief can cause a child to act along the grief band for a short while, so can a 0.5 fixation cause an individual to act 0.5 toward most things in his life.

There is momentary behavior or fixed behavior.

How can one find an individual on this Tone Scale?

How can one find oneself?

If you can locate two or three characteristics along a certain level of this scale, you can look in the number column opposite those characteristics and find the level. It may be 2.5, it may be 1.5. Wherever it is, simply look at *all* the columns opposite the number you found and you will see the remaining characteristics.

The only mistake you can make in evaluating somebody else on this Tone Scale is to assume that he departs from it somewhere and is higher in one department than he is in another. The characteristic to which you object may be masked—but it is there.

Look at the top of the first column and you get a general picture of the behavior and physiology of the person. Look at the second column for the physical condition. Look at the third column for the most generally expressed emotion of the person. Continue on across the various columns. Somewhere you will find data about somebody or yourself of which you can be sure. Then simply examine all the other boxes at the level of the data you were certain about. That band, be it 1.5 or 3.0, will tell you the story of a human being.

Of course, as good news and bad, happy days and sad ones strike a person, there are momentary rises and lowerings on this Tone Scale. But there is a chronic level, an average behavior for each individual.

As an individual is found lower and lower on this chart, so is his alertness, his consciousness lower and lower.

The individual's chronic mood or attitude toward existence declines in direct ratio to the way he regards the physical universe and organisms about him.

There are many other mechanical aspects of this chart having to do with energy manifestations and observation of behavior, but we need not cover them here.

It is not a complete statement to say, merely, that one becomes fixed in his regard for the physical universe and organisms about him. For there are definite ways, beyond consciousness, which permit this to take place. Manifestation, however, is a decline of consciousness with regard to the physical environment of an individual. That decline of consciousness is a partial cause of a gradual sag down this chart, but it is illustrative enough for our purposes in this volume.

At the top of this chart, one is fully conscious of himself, his environment, other people and the universe in general. He accepts his responsibilities in it. He faces the realities of it. He deals with the problems within the limits of his education and experience.

Then something happens—his perception of the material universe is dulled. How does this come about?

The first and foremost way that a decline on the chart is begun is through being caused physical pain by the physical universe. It is one thing to gain experience and quite another to suffer physical pain. For any experience surrounded by actual physical pain is *hidden* by that pain. The organism is supposed to avoid pain to survive. It avoids, as well, memories of pain if it is above 2.0 on the chart. It "relishes" pain memories below 2.0 as these lead to death. As soon as it can begin avoiding pain wholesale, although that pain is recorded, consciousness begins to decrease markedly. The perception of the physical universe begins to decrease and the caliber of one's activities begins to decline.

One could say that there is an interior world and an exterior world. The interior world is the one of yesterday. The data it contains is used to judge the world of the exterior of today and tomorrow.

So long as one has all data available, one can make excellent computations. When the facts he has learned begin to be buried, one's conclusions are apt to become wrong to just that degree.

As one's confidence in the physical universe declines, so does one's ability to handle it decline. One's dreams and hopes begin to seem unattainable, one ceases to strive. Actually, however, one's ability seldom diminishes—it only *seems* to diminish.

When the interior world tells of too much physical pain, the organism becomes confused. Like the child who finally says he doesn't want the nickel, the organism says it wants nothing of the physical universe and so perishes—or lives a while in a twilight and then perishes all the same.

The goal is to win. When one has lost too much and too many times, the possibility of winning *seems* too remote to try. And one loses. He becomes so accustomed to loss that he begins to concentrate on loss instead of forward advance. And he does this quite irrationally. Because one has lost two cars does not mean one may lose three. Yet he who has lost two will actually be so prepared to lose three that he will actually, if unconsciously, take steps to lose the third. Thus it may be with people, with any object.

As an individual descends the Tone Scale, he first begins to lose his confidence in trying to reach the further rims of his environment, the further frontiers of his dreams, and becomes conservative. There is not much wrong with cautiousness, but there is something wrong with chronic conservatism. For sometimes it takes a wild charge to win a life.

As physical pain begins to mount up in the recording banks of the mind, the individual further confuses yesterday with today and further withdraws his confidence. He becomes a little frightened and poses as being bored. He says he didn't want to reach so far anyway—isn't worth it. He makes fun of the things he really wants, makes fun of the dreams of others and acts, in general, like a reporter from the *New Yorker*. He is afraid to face a hopeful fact, much less a truly desirable object.

With a further increase of pain, he continues on down the scale until he is actually on his way out from life.

The fact of the matter is, the older a person gets and the more experiences he has, the better able he should be to handle his environment. If he could stay fully conscious and rational about it, this would be true. But the mechanics of pain storage are such that he actually grows less and less conscious, the more pain he has received, and so cannot really use his experience at all. If he could gain experience without physical pain, his enthusiasm, his ability and dash would remain very high. But Man was a lesser organism, evidently, before he was a man. And a lesser organism can only react, it cannot think. Thinking is something new.

Until Dianetics, this looked like a hopelessly closed cycle. One had enthusiasm but no experience. So with enthusiastic rushes he attacked the environment with all the folly of youth and was ignominiously repelled. He gained pain with each repulsion. He gained experience, but he could not think about the experience without facing the pain so the experience did him no good. When he had enough experience, he no longer had the dreams, energy and enthusiasm to carry home his attack upon his environment.

Processing—such as the questions in Chapter Ten of this book or in Dianetic co-auditing—broke the cycle. Youth could attack the environment and experience pain of repulsion. But the physical pain could be knocked out of the mind, by Dianetics, leaving the experience standing there *with* the enthusiasm.

There must be, at this writing, tens of thousands of people who have experienced Dianetics by now. A few, here and there, were unable to achieve full benefit because it formerly required considerable technical knowledge to process somebody. This book and Self Analysis were developed in order that an individual could gain at least the primary benefits of processing without any technical knowledge and without taking up the time of another person.

Wherever a person may be on the Tone Scale (unless he is very low and in the insane bracket, for this is also a scale of sanity) he can ascend that scale again by rehabilitating his ability to think about and know his environment. Now that one knows the rules it is rather easily done and one is astonished that it could not be done before.

Have you looked at the chart for yourself? Well, don't go looking for a cliff or an ax if you were below 2.0. Self Analysis can pull you up this chart so that even you will see that you have climbed.

Now, just beyond the chart there are some tests and graphs. You should answer these. They will help you to locate yourself. Then you will know much better why you are or aren't a good friend to yourself. You may find you don't care to have such a friend. Well, if he's that bad off, he really needs your help. So give him a hand. The whole last part of the book is filled with exercises which will make a better friend to have out of yourself if you just apply these exercises a half an hour a day.

I don't know how high you can get yourself up on this chart. You can raise yourself pretty far and Dianetic co-auditing can do the rest if you wish. Or you may get all the way and stabilize there.

Right now, if you aren't being a friend of yourself, I'm your friend. I know by experience that you can climb the chart.

Man is basically good. Pain and social aberrations turn him away from high ethics, efficiency and happiness. Get rid of the pain and you'll be at the high level of the chart.

Now turn to the questions which will help you locate yourself.

BUT DON'T USE THIS CHART AS AN EFFORT TO MAKE SOMEBODY KNUCKLE UNDER. DON'T TELL PEOPLE WHERE THEY ARE ON IT. IT MAY RUIN THEM. LET THEM TAKE THEIR OWN EXAMINATIONS.

THE HUBBARD
CHART OF HUMAN
EVALUATION

THE HUBBARD CHART OF HUMAN EVALUATION

T his chart is a specialized form of the Hubbard Chart of Human Evaluation and Dianetic Processing.

A full description of each column on this chart (except the last six, which are only in *Self Analysis*) will be found complete in *Science of Survival*.

The technical name of the questioning process used in this volume is *Dianetic Straightwire* with emphasis on *Validation MEST Processing*. This is actually not "self-auditing." It is auditing done on the reader by the author. Actually, the reader is being audited by L. Ron Hubbard. Straightwire Processing is relatively safe on any case and is the most elementary process in Dianetics.

The position of an individual on this Tone Scale varies through the day and throughout the years, but is fairly stable for given periods. One's position on the chart will rise on receipt of good news, sink with bad news. This is the usual give-and-take with life. Everyone, however, has a *chronic* position on the chart which is unalterable, save for processing.

Necessity level (lifting oneself by one's bootstraps, as in emergencies) can raise an individual well up this chart for brief periods.

By education, such as that given under pressure, the education itself has a position on the Tone Scale. A person could be relatively unaberrated actually but, by education, be at a lower position on the chart than he should be. The reverse is also the case. One can be educated, then, into a higher or lower level on the chart than his own aberrations call for.

One's environment greatly influences one's position on the chart. Every environment has its own tone level. A man who is really a 3.0 can begin to act like a 1.1 in a 1.1 environment. However, a 1.1 usually acts no better than about 1.5 in an environment with a high tone. If one lives in a low-toned environment, he can expect eventually to be low toned. This is also true of marriage—one tends to match the tone level of one's marital partner.

This Tone Scale is also valid for groups. A business or a nation can be examined as to its various standard reactions and these can be plotted. This will give the survival potential of a business or a nation.

This chart can also be used in employing people or in choosing partners. It is an accurate index of what to expect and gives you a chance to predict what people will do before you have any great experience with them. Also, it gives you some clue as to what can happen to you in certain environments or around certain people, for they can drag you down or boost you high.

THE HUBBARD CHART
OF HUMAN EVALUATION[*]

*A foldout version of this chart is
contained at the back of this book.*

---

[*] A more extensive version of this chart and full description of the columns appear in the book
Science of Survival.

TONE SCALE		**1** BEHAVIOR AND PHYSIOLOGY	**2** MEDICAL RANGE	**3** EMOTION
	4.0	Excellent at projects, execution. Fast reaction time (relative to age).	Near accident-proof. No psychosomatic ills. Nearly immune to bacteria.	Exhilaration. ——— Eagerness.
	3.5	Good at projects, execution, sports.	Highly resistant to common infections—no colds.	Strong interest. ——— Mild interest.
	3.0	Capable of fair amount of action, sports.	Resistant to infection and disease. Few psychosomatic ills.	Content.
	2.5	Relatively inactive but capable of action.	Occasionally ill. Susceptible to usual diseases.	Indifference. ——— Boredom.
	2.0	Capable of destructive and minor constructive action.	Severe sporadic illnesses.	Expressed resentment.
	1.5	Capable of destructive action.	Depository illnesses (arthritis). (Range 1.0 to 2.0 interchangeable.)	Anger.
	1.1	Capable of minor execution.	Endocrine and neurological illnesses.	Unexpressed resentment. ——— Fear.
	0.5	Capable of relatively uncontrolled action.	Chronic malfunction of organs. (Accident-prone.)	Grief. ——— Apathy.
	0.1	Alive as an organism.	Chronically ill. (Refusing sustenance.)	Deepest apathy. ——— None.

4 SEXUAL BEHAVIOR ATTITUDE TOWARD CHILDREN	5 COMMAND OVER ENVIRONMENT	6 ACTUAL WORTH TO SOCIETY COMPARED TO APPARENT WORTH		
Sexual interest high but often sublimated to creative thought. ——— Intense interest in children.	High self-mastery. Aggressive toward environ. Dislikes to control people. High reasoning, volatile emotions.	High worth. Apparent worth will be realized. Creative and constructive.	4.0	TONE SCALE
High interest in opposite sex. Constancy. ——— Love of children.	Reasons well. Good control. Accepts ownership. Emotion free. Liberal.	Good value to society. Adjusts environ to benefit of self and others.	3.5	
Interest in procreation. ——— Interest in children.	Controls bodily functions. Reasons well. Free emotion still inhibited. Allows rights to others. Democratic.	Any apparent worth is actual worth. Fair value.	3.0	
Disinterest in procreation. ——— Vague tolerance of children.	In control of functions and some reasoning powers. Does not desire ownership of much.	Capable of constructive action, seldom any quantity to be reckoned with. Small value. "Well adjusted."	2.5	
Disgust for sex—revulsion. ——— Nagging of, nervousness about children.	Antagonistic and destructive to self, others and environ. Desires command in order to injure.	Dangerous. Any apparent worth wiped out by potentials of injury to others.	2.0	
Rape, sex as punishment. ——— Brutal treatment of children.	Smashes or destroys others or environment. Failing, may destroy self. Fascistic.	Insincere. Heavy liability. Possible murderer. Even when intentions avowedly good will bring about destruction.	1.5	
Promiscuity, perversion, sadism, irregular practices. ——— Use of children for sadistic purposes.	No control of reason or emotions, but apparent organic control. Uses sly means of controlling others, especially hypnotism. Communistic.	Active liability. Enturbulates others. Apparent worth outweighed by vicious, hidden intents.	1.1	
Impotency, anxiety, possible efforts to procreate. ——— Anxiety about children.	Barest functional control of self, only. No control of reason or emotions.	Liability to society. Possible suicide. Utterly careless of others.	0.5	
No effort to procreate.	No command of self, environment, other persons. Suicide.	High liability, needing care and efforts of others without any contribution.	0.1	

		7 ETHIC LEVEL	8 HANDLING OF TRUTH	9 COURAGE LEVEL
TONE SCALE	4.0	Bases ethics on reason. Very high ethic level.	High concept of truth.	High courage level.
	3.5	Heeds ethics of group but refines them higher as reason demands.	Truthful.	Courage displayed on reasonable risks.
	3.0	Follows ethics in which trained, as honestly as possible. Moral.	Cautious of asserting truths. Social lies.	Conservative display of courage where risk is small.
	2.5	Treats ethics insincerely but not particularly honest or dishonest.	Insincere. Careless of facts.	Neither courage nor cowardice. Neglect of danger.
	2.0	Chronically and bluntly dishonest when occasion arises. At this level and below: authoritarianism, criminals.	Truth twisted to suit antagonism.	Reactive, unreasoning thrusts at danger.
	1.5	Immoral. Actively dishonest. Destructive of any and all ethics.	Blatant and destructive lying.	Unreasonable bravery, usually damaging to self.
	1.1	Sex criminals. Negative ethics. Deviously dishonest. Perverts honesty without reason.	Ingenious and vicious perversions of truth. Covers lying artfully.	Occasional underhanded displays of action, otherwise cowardly.
	0.5	Non-existent. Not thinking. Obeying anyone.	Details facts with no concept of their reality.	Complete cowardice.
	0.1	None.	No reaction.	No reaction.

10 SPEECH: Talks / SPEECH: Listens	11 SUBJECT'S HANDLING OF WRITTEN OR SPOKEN COMM WHEN ACTING AS A RELAY POINT	12 REALITY (AGREEMENT)	TONE SCALE
Strong, able, swift and full exchange of beliefs, ideas.	Passes theta comm, contributes to it. Cuts entheta lines.	Search for different viewpoints in order to broaden own reality. Changes reality.	4.0
Will talk of deep-seated beliefs and ideas. Will accept deep-seated ideas, beliefs and consider them.	Passes theta comm. Resents and hits back at entheta lines.	Ability to understand and evaluate reality of others and to change viewpoint. Agreeable.	3.5
Tentative expression of limited number of personal ideas. Receives ideas and beliefs if cautiously stated.	Passes comm. Conservative. Inclines toward moderate construction and creation.	Awareness of possible validity of different reality. Conservative agreement.	3.0
Casual, pointless conversation. Listens only to ordinary affairs.	Cancels any comm of higher or lower tone—devaluates urgencies.	Refusal to match two realities. Indifference to conflicts in reality. Too careless to agree or disagree.	2.5
Talks in threats. Invalidates other people. Listens to threats. Openly mocks theta talk.	Deals in hostile or threatening comm. Lets only small amount of theta go through.	Verbal doubt—defense of own reality. Attempts to undermine others'. Disagrees.	2.0
Talks of death and destruction only. Hate. Listens only to death and destruction. Wrecks theta lines.	Perverts comm to entheta regardless of original content. Stops theta comm. Passes entheta and perverts it.	Destruction of opposing reality. "You're wrong." Disagrees with reality of others.	1.5
Talks in apparent theta but vicious intent. Lies. Listens little but mostly to cabal or gossip. Lies.	Relays only malicious comm. Cuts comm lines. Won't relay comm.	Doubt of own reality. Insecurity. Doubt of opposing reality.	1.1
Talks only in apathetic tones. Very little. Listens little, mostly to apathy or pity.	Takes little heed of communications. Does not pass them.	Shame, anxiety—strong doubt of own reality, easily has reality of others forced on him.	0.5
Does not talk. Does not listen.	Does not relay communications. Unaware of them.	Complete withdrawal from conflicting reality—no reality.	0.1

TONE SCALE		13 ABILITY TO HANDLE RESPONSIBILITY	14 PERSISTENCE ON A GIVEN COURSE	15 LITERALNESS OF RECEPTION OF STATEMENTS
	4.0	Inherent sense of responsibility on all dynamics.	High creative persistence.	High differentiation. Good understanding of all comm as modified by Clear's education.
	3.5	Capable of assuming and carrying on responsibilities.	Good persistence and direction toward constructive goals.	Good grasp of statements. Good sense of humor.
	3.0	Handles responsibility in a slipshod fashion.	Fair persistence if obstacles not too great.	Good differentiation of meaning of statements.
	2.5	Very careless, not trustworthy.	Idle, poor concentration.	Accepts very little, literally or otherwise. Apt to be literal about humor.
	2.0	Uses responsibility to further own ends.	Persistence toward destruction of enemies. No constructive persistence below this point.	Accepts remarks of Tone 2.0 literally.
	1.5	Assumes responsibility in order to destroy.	Destructive persistence begins strongly, weakens quickly.	Accepts alarming remarks literally. Brutal sense of humor.
	1.1	Incapable, capricious, irresponsible.	Vacillation on any course. Very poor concentration. Flighty.	Lack of acceptance of any remarks. Tendency to accept all literally avoided by forced humor.
	0.5	None.	Sporadic persistence toward self-destruction.	Literal acceptance of any remark matching tone.
	0.1	None.	None.	Complete literal acceptance.

	16 METHOD USED BY SUBJECT TO HANDLE OTHERS	17 HYPNOTIC LEVEL	18 ABILITY TO EXPERIENCE PRESENT TIME PLEASURE	
	Gains support by creative enthusiasm and vitality backed by reason.	Impossible to hypnotize without drugs and consent.	Finds existence very full of pleasure.	**4.0** TONE SCALE
	Gains support by creative reasoning and vitality.	Difficult to trance unless still possessed of a trance engram.	Finds life pleasurable most of the time.	**3.5**
	Invites support by practical reasoning and social graces.	Could be hypnotized, but alert when awake.	Experiences pleasure some of the time.	**3.0**
	Careless of support from others.	Can be a hypnotic subject, but mostly alert.	Sometimes experiences a moment of pleasure. Low intensity.	**2.5**
	Nags and bluntly criticizes to demand compliance with wishes.	Negates somewhat, but can be hypnotized.	Occasionally experiences some pleasure in extraordinary moments.	**2.0**
	Uses threats, punishment and alarming lies to dominate others.	Negates heavily against remarks, but absorbs them.	Seldom experiences any pleasure.	**1.5**
	Nullifies others to get them to level where they can be used. Devious and vicious means. Hypnotism, gossip. Seeks hidden control.	In a permanent light trance, but negates.	Most gaiety forced. Real pleasure out of reach.	**1.1**
	Enturbulates others to control them. Cries for pity. Wild lying to gain sympathy.	Very hypnotic. Any remark made may be a "positive suggestion."	None.	**0.5**
	Pretends death so others will not think him dangerous and will go away.	Is equivalent to a hypnotized subject when "awake."	None.	**0.1**

		19 YOUR VALUE AS A FRIEND	20 HOW MUCH OTHERS LIKE YOU	21 STATE OF YOUR POSSESSIONS
TONE SCALE	4.0	Excellent.	Loved by many.	In excellent condition.
	3.5	Very good.	Well loved.	In good condition.
	3.0	Good.	Respected by most.	Fairly good.
	2.5	Fair.	Liked by a few.	Shows some neglect.
	2.0	Poor.	Rarely liked.	Very neglected.
	1.5	Definite liability.	Openly disliked by most.	Often broken. Bad repair.
	1.1	Dangerous liability.	Generally despised.	Poor. In poor condition.
	0.5	Very great liability.	Not liked. Only pitied by some.	In very bad condition generally.
	0.1	Total liability.	Not regarded.	No realization of possession.

22 How Well Are You Understood	23 Potential Success	24 Potential Survival	Tone Scale
Very well.	Excellent.	Excellent. Considerable longevity.	4.0
Well.	Very good.	Very good.	3.5
Usually.	Good.	Good.	3.0
Sometimes misunderstood.	Fair.	Fair.	2.5
Often misunderstood.	Poor.	Poor.	2.0
Continually misunderstood.	Usually a failure.	Early demise.	1.5
No real understanding.	Nearly always fails.	Brief.	1.1
Not at all understood.	Utter failure.	Demise soon.	0.5
Ignored.	No effort. Complete failure.	Almost dead.	0.1

TONE SCALE TESTS

TONE SCALE TESTS

TEST NUMBER ONE

Take this test before you begin on the Processing Section of *Self Analysis.*

Be fair and as honest as possible in your findings.

Use, as a basis, how you have been in the last year. Earlier conditions in your life do not count.

Open up chart* to column 1, Behavior and Physiology. Ask yourself how active you are physically. Locate the place in this column which most nearly seems to fit you.

Look on the Tone Scale for the number of the square you have found. Is it 3.0? Is it 2.5?

Take this number and go to the graph on the following page.

Under column 1, as marked at the top of the graph, locate the number (3.0, 2.5 or whatever it was) and place an *X* in this square. This gives the same place on the graph that you found on the chart.

Go to column 2 on the chart, Medical Range.

Find the square which best describes your health. Note the number given in the Tone Scale column opposite the square you have chosen. (3.5, 2.0 or whatever it was.)

Turn back to the graph of Test One. In column 2 on the graph, put an *X* opposite the Tone Scale number you got from the chart.

---

* A foldout version of this chart is contained at the back of this book.

Carry through this process with all columns until you have an *X* in each column of the graph. Omit the last six.

Take a straightedge or ruler. Move it on the graph, holding it horizontally, until you have the level of the graph which contains the most *X*s. Draw a line through these *X*s all the way across the chart and out to the edge. This line will give you your position in the last six columns.

The horizontal line you have just drawn gives you your position on the Tone Scale. This level of the chart is yours.

Leave this graph in the book. Keep it so that you can compare it in a few weeks when you do Test Two.

Note that in columns 4 and 10 the squares are divided in the same manner as the squares on the chart. You make two evaluations of yourself for these columns and you put an *X* in a half square, using two half squares for each column, even if one *X* falls at 3.0 and the other *X* falls at 1.1.

TONE SCALE	1	2	3	4	5	6	7	8	9	10	11	12	13	14	15	16	17	18	19	20	21	22	23	24	TONE SCALE
4.0																									4.0
3.5																									3.5
3.0																									3.0
2.5																									2.5
2.0																									2.0
1.5																									1.5
1.1																									1.1
0.5																									0.5
0.1																									0.1

TEST NUMBER TWO

Take this test after you have been processing yourself about two weeks, or about fifteen hours.

Use as your data how you have felt about things since taking Test One.

TONE SCALE	1	2	3	4	5	6	7	8	9	10	11	12	13	14	15	16	17	18	19	20	21	22	23	24	TONE SCALE
4.0																									4.0
3.5																									3.5
3.0																									3.0
2.5																									2.5
2.0																									2.0
1.5																									1.5
1.1																									1.1
0.5																									0.5
0.1																									0.1

TEST NUMBER THREE

Use this test after you have been processing yourself two months.

Use as data how you have felt about things since taking the second test.

Use the same directions as given in Test One.

CHAPTER EIGHT
TONE SCALE TESTS

TONE SCALE	1	2	3	4	5	6	7	8	9	10	11	12	13	14	15	16	17	18	19	20	21	22	23	24	TONE SCALE
4.0																									4.0
3.5																									3.5
3.0																									3.0
2.5																									2.5
2.0																									2.0
1.5																									1.5
1.1																									1.1
0.5																									0.5
0.1																									0.1

HOW TO
USE THE DISK

How to Use the Disk

I M P O R T A N T

 slotted disk is provided for the reader's use. The disk must be used. Without using the disk, the benefit of processing is cut more than 80 percent.

The disk is placed over question 1 of a list so that the question shows through. One recalls the incident desired.

Then one looks at the uppermost word on the disk itself. This says, for instance, "Sight."

One seeks to "see," in recall, the incident desired.

One tries, then, to recall another incident without moving the disk. He then seeks to "see" this incident in recalling it.

One tries to recall, then, the earliest incident of this kind he can and seeks to "see" this one.

Then one drops the disk one question, rotating it at the same time so that another "sense" appears at the top. He uses this "sense" particularly in recalling the incident.

Turn the disk over on each new page, so that a new set of perceptions comes up.

It does not matter what "sense" you begin to recall with. It does not matter which side you first begin to use.

Eventually you should be able to get more and more perceptions on any one incident until, at last, you may recover all of them without strain.

If you lose the disk, the full list of perceptions on it are at the side of every page. Take a pencil and check them off one at a time just as though they were appearing on the disk.

A green disk and a white disk are provided. Use the one you like best.

IF YOU ONLY GET A VAGUE CONCEPT OF WHAT THE SENSE MUST HAVE BEEN LIKE, IF YOU DO NOT AT FIRST GET ACTUAL RECALL BY THE SENSE ITSELF, BE SURE THAT YOU AT LEAST GET A CONCEPTION OF IT.

DIANETIC PROCESSING

Dianetic Processing may be divided into two classes.

The first is *Light Processing.* This includes analytical recall of conscious moments. It is intended to raise tone and increase perception and memory. It often resolves chronic somatics (psychosomatic ills).

The second is *Deep Processing.* This addresses basic cause and locates and reduces moments of physical pain and sorrow. It is done, without drugs or hypnosis, by an *auditor* (one who listens and computes). Auditors have either learned Dianetics after a thorough study of the basic text *Science of Survival* or they have been trained professionally at the Hubbard Dianetic Foundation.[*]

This book contains Light Processing. This book is not "self-auditing." "Self-auditing" is nearly impossible. In this book, the author, L. Ron Hubbard, is actually giving the reader Light Processing.

---

[*] See *Addresses* listed at the back of this book.

PROCESSING SECTION

PROCESSING SECTION

H ere begin the lists of questions by which the individual can explore his past and improve his reactions toward life. Dianetically speaking, this self-processing section could be called *Straightwire*. It is not "auto-processing." The reader is actually being processed by the author.

In the full use of Dianetics, these questions could be considered as preparatory to co-auditing. The auditor is assisted by these lists in that they open a case for the running of engrams and secondaries and raise the preclear on a Tone Scale. These question sections, so far as is known at this time, will not run out engrams and secondaries as such, but will desensitize them to a marked extent with a consequent improvement in the mental and physical being of the individual.

An auditor—as the practitioner in Dianetics is called, since he both listens and computes—can use these questions during a session with a preclear. Further, two people can work with these sections—one of them asking the questions of another who answers, or both of them reading the questions and both of them attempting to get a recall on such an incident as that one called for.

These lists are used repetitively. That is to say, the individual goes over them again and again. There is no finite period to the work. The reason the recall of these questions is important is that they reveal and discharge *locks* which have formed above the basic *engrams* (moments of physical pain and unconsciousness) and *secondaries* (moments of acute loss as death of a loved one). The discharging of these locks renders engrams and secondaries relatively ineffective. A full Dianetic clearing of the individual's engrams and secondaries gives the highest possible attainable results. But these questions provide self-processing which prepares the case for such an action and are in themselves highly beneficial.

In the process of using these questions the preclear may discover many manifestations in himself. He may experience considerable emotional release. He may become angry at the recollection of some of the things which have happened to him. And he may even feel like crying over some of the losses he has sustained and, indeed, may very well cry. However, the intent of these questions is not to focus the self-processor's attention upon the bad things which have happened to him, but upon the good things which have taken place in his life. A concentration upon these happier circumstances tends to discharge the unhappy circumstances and render them far less forceful.

These questions are based upon the Dianetic discoveries, axioms and postulates which have done so much toward amplifying the understanding of people concerning the nature of existence and their roles in it.

Life can be considered to have as its fundamental purpose survival in the material universe. When one closely examines survival, he discovers that the concept embraces all the activities of an individual, a group, a state, life itself or the material universe.

The material universe is composed of matter, energy, space and time.

Life can, then, be considered to be engaged upon the conquest of matter, energy, space and time, including other life forms, organisms and persons. If an organism or a group has been successful in handling other organisms, groups and the material universe, its survival potential is very great. If the organism has been unsuccessful, its survival potential is lower. Its moments of success, as its moments of pain, are highly charged.

It is possible, by certain processes, to remove the charge from painful incidents. One of the ways of doing this is to lay the stress and concentration of the organism upon the times it has been successful in surviving.

With the invention of language, Man brought upon himself an unexpected source of aberration. While language itself is very far from the whole reason an organism is less successful than it might be, our current social order lays undue stress upon language. Words are only symbols which represent actions. A child learns these actions very early and learns the symbols which represent the actions. Later on, he begins to mistake the action for the symbol and begins to believe the words themselves have force and power—which they do not. If you believe that words have force and power, hold your hand in front of your mouth and say a few words. You will see how negligible is the force of utterance, no matter what words you use.

Underlying this mistaken emphasis on the force of words lie actual physical actions of which the words are the symbols. The main point, then, is that words are not powerful but actions are. For example, when an individual has been told to hold still, he obeys simply because he has experienced earlier in his life the action of being made to hold still by physical force.

For many reasons it is important for the organism to increase its mobility. The discovery of all the times the organism has been told to hold still and has obeyed has some therapeutic value. But the discovery of actual incidents when the organism has been physically forced to remain motionless is much more important in restoring the mobility of the organism.

These lists, then, tend to devaluate the importance of language. This is only one of their many functions, but an important one. Therefore, the reading of these lists should direct the individual to moments action took place, not when somebody said it took place. Just as hearsay evidence is not admissible in a court of law, so are words and phrases given to the individual by others inadmissible in self-processing.

For instance, when one is asked for a time when somebody went away, one should not try to recall the time when somebody said somebody went away or the statement that somebody was going away, but the actual physical departure—regardless of what was said.

You will find that words are communicated through the physical universe to other organisms. Sounds, for instance, originate within the organism, are translated into sound waves and reach the other person as sound waves. The written word is made into symbols of ink, which are then seen (the other physical fact of light) by another organism. Whereas there may very well be such things as ESP, it is not aberrative.

There are many perceptions—which is to say, channels—through which one can contact the physical universe. You are aware of the physical universe because of sight, sound, mouth and other message systems. Therefore, each time you are asked to recall an incident of a certain kind, you will be asked—after you have recalled it—to pay attention to a certain sense channel which was present during the time when you experienced the incident.

The circular disk is provided for this purpose. You will notice the disk has two sides. The perceptions or sense messages listed on one side are different from those on the other side. As you read the questions one after the other, you should read them through a slot provided in this disk. Going to the next question, you should rotate the slot once counterclockwise for each new question. This will give you a new perception.

For instance, the question may pertain to a time somebody went away from you. You will recall a time when this occurred, selecting the moment of actual physical departure. Undoubtedly, you will get some perception of the scene and you may even get a very full perception of the scene. Many people see, feel, hear and otherwise perceive memories when they recall them. Some people are too occluded. These lists wipe away occlusion. As you recall the person walking away from you, then, you are not supposed to recall merely the concept that somebody had walked away, but the moment when they actually did—and get as many perceptions as possible of them doing so. The disk which overlies this question will have uppermost, at random, one particular perception. That perception may be "Sound." Thus you should attempt to recover whatever sounds were present when this individual walked away as the particular emphasis of perception. *If you are unable to recover the sounds as such, hearing them again, at least recover the concept of what they may have been.*

If you will examine this disk, you will find that it lists six perceptions with which you have contacted the physical universe. Actually, there are many more of these than six.

When the word "Emotion" is uppermost above a question, after you have recalled the incident suggested by the question you then try to recall, in particular, and feel again, if possible, the emotion you felt at the time.

When the next question is addressed, the disk is rotated one turn counterclockwise. You will find that "Loudness" is now uppermost. You should get an incident in recall suggested by the question and, having perceived the incident, you should then give your attention in particular to the loudness of the various sounds in the incident.

Going to the next question, you should rotate the disk once more counterclockwise. You will find that "Body Position" is now uppermost. You should read the question and recall some incident it suggests, perceive it as well as you possibly can and then give particular attention to the position your own body was in at the time the incident occurred.

Going to the next question and rotating the disk once more, you will find that "Sound" is now uppermost. You should recall the incident the question calls for and then give particular attention to the sounds in that incident.

Going to the next question and rotating the disk once more, you will find that "Weight" is uppermost. In the incident you recall, you should then give attention to the heaviness of things, including the pull of gravity on yourself and the weight of anything you may actually be supporting in the incident, such as your clothes, a ball or any other thing which you are actually holding at the time the incident occurred.

Rotating the disk once more to the next question on the list, you will find that "Personal Motion" falls uppermost. When you have answered the question, then you should give attention to the motion which you yourself were undertaking at the time the incident occurred.

Every time you go to a new page you should turn the disk upside down. You will find here a new set of perceptics.

These, of course, are applied in such a way that when you go over the list a second time you will probably not have the same perception, as these things fall at random. Thus, while you might have answered a question the first time about somebody coming toward you with attention to "Sound" called for by the disk, the next time you reach this question (on going over the list again) you may find "Emotion" uppermost. You should then contact any and all emotion on the second time, whereas you contacted the sound the first time.

You will find on the reverse side of the disk the perceptions of "Sight," "Smell," "Touch," "Color," "Tone" and "External Motion."

"Sight" is what you actually saw at the time. A person whose perceptions are in good condition will see again what he has seen before when the incident actually occurred. Thus "Sight" calls for what was seen while the incident called for was taking place.

"Smell" requests the individual to recall any and all odors which were present during the scene he is recalling.

"Touch" requests the recall of anything the individual was actually touching at the time with the sensation of touch, including pressure. One is always in contact with the material world in terms of touch, even if only the touch of his feet on the ground or the feel of his clothes upon him.

The perception of "Color," when uppermost, should cause the individual to try to perceive again the color which was contained in the scene called for.

When "Tone" is requested, the individual should attempt to contact the quality of the sound present when the scene occurred.

When "External Motion" is uppermost, the individual, in recalling the incident called for by the question, should attempt to perceive in the incident recalled the movement contained in the incident—the motion of other people or objects or of energy.

As one goes over these questions, then, with the disk, he is exploring his own life and during that exploration is attempting to call into view with the highest possible level of reality those things he has perceived. The immediate result is a heightening of perception of his present time world. Another result is a strengthening of his memory. Yet another result is the rearrangement and reevaluation of things which have happened to him. Another and more mechanical and fundamental result is the deintensification of unpleasant experiences—like bringing them into the light. For a while, one may feel it is better to forget unpleasant things. Forgotten, they have more force and destructive quality than when examined.

The individual will find himself, as he repeatedly uses a list, getting earlier and earlier incidents. It is not impossible for him to remember straight back to the earliest beginnings of his life, much less his infancy.

Again, and it cannot be emphasized too strongly, these questions are requesting actual physical actions, not statements about physical actions. It is perfectly legitimate to recall scenes which have been seen in the movies or read about in books. But when one recalls such scenes, one should have full awareness, in the case of the movies, of the screen and the seat and where the incident is taking place and when. In the case of books, one should get not the scene the author would like the reader to see, but the actual scene of reading—and the recall should be recaptured in terms of print and sitting in a chair, not in terms of imagining.

There is a great deal of technology, out of sight, back of these questions. All that is important is that this operation, continued persistently, going over one list and then another and recalling the things required, considerably improves the individual's thinking and acting abilities and his physical well-being and considerably enhances his relationship with his present environment.

You will find the very last list is named the "End of Session List." This means that after you have worked a list, or worked as long as you desire to during any one period of self-processing, you should turn to the "End of Session List" and answer the questions as a routine operation.

You will also find a list entitled "If Recalling a Certain Thing Made You Uncomfortable," which is placed next to the last in the book. If you find during a session of self-processing that you grow considerably uncomfortable or unhappy, you should then turn to this list. Using it should restore your good spirit swiftly.

If you find it is extremely difficult to recall any one question in these lists, simply pass over it and go to the next question. If you find you are having difficulty in answering any of these lists, you will do better if some friend reads them to you.

If undergoing self-processing makes you extremely unhappy, it is probable that your case should be given the attention of a Dianetic auditor until such time as you are capable of handling this matter for yourself.

You can go over a list many times before going on to the next list or you can continue on through all of the lists consecutively without repeating any. You will probably find that going over each list many times before going on to the next will work better than going through the book consecutively.

You will notice that after you have been over the same memory several times, even though it be an unpleasant one, that it will cease to have any effect upon you. This means its intensity is decreasing and that the energy which it contained and which was affecting your present time life is dissipating. If you can remember several incidents of the same kind, do so. And if they are troublesome to you, simply go over the things you remembered once more, one after the other, and then again. This, Dianetically speaking, is called *Repetitive Straightwire*. It deintensifies unpleasant memories. However, these lists are aimed toward the recall of pleasant incidents. Pleasant incidents do not deintensify as unpleasant ones do but, underneath the level of attention, deintensify unpleasant incidents when the pleasant incident is recalled.

All you really need to work these lists is to know that actions, not words, are required and that the disk should be used to give you the particular kind of recall you should have on the recollection called for. If you lose the disk, you will note that the side of the page has a list of the perceptions for your reference. When using the side-of-the-page list, you should merely take the recalls, the perceptions, consecutively one after the other and use them the same way you used them with the disk.

Don't simply answer questions "Yes" or "No." Select an actual moment in your life called for by the question. Try to re-sense that moment with the perceptic called for on the disk.

If going over the questions makes you unhappy, simply continue with the list you are working, over and over. The unhappiness should "wear out" after unhappy incidents are recalled many times. The feeling will turn to one of relief.

Some people are frightened at the idea of persevering with these questions. Certainly you've got more nerve than that. The worst they could do is kill you.

Don't be surprised if you feel sleepy after using some of these questions. The sleepiness is only a symptom of relaxing. The very least this book can do for you is replace your sedatives!

If, while answering these questions, you begin to yawn, that is good. Yawning is a release of former periods of unconsciousness. You may yawn so much the tears come out of your eyes. That is progress.

Should you feel very groggy while answering these questions, that is only "boil-off," the manifestation of former periods of unconsciousness boiling-off. Simply persist in recalling the incident or others like it and the feeling will pass away, leaving you more alert than before. If you interrupt this boil-off and stop your session, you may feel cross or irritable. This grogginess occasionally amounts to nearly complete unconsciousness, but it always goes away. That unconsciousness was what was keeping you from being high on the Tone Scale.

Occasionally vague or even sharp pains may turn on and off as you are answering questions. Don't try to find out where they came from. They will go away if you persist with these questions. Simply ignore them. They are the ghosts of what they used to call psychosomatic ills, former injuries restimulated.

An individual is suppressed by these deposits of past pain and unconsciousness. Self Analysis makes such past moments pass away and deintensify, at least partially, without your having to find out what was in them.

A full description of these manifestations and their causes occur in Science of Survival, *the popular text on Dianetics.*

USE LISTS MANY TIMES. Try for the earliest incident you can get for each question.

GENERAL
INCIDENTS

T he purpose of this list is to give you practice in recalling things. Use the disk provided in the back of the book and look at the beginning of this section for instructions as to how this list is to be used.

Can you recall a time when:

1. You were happy.

2. You had just finished constructing something.

3. Life was cheerful.

4. Somebody had given you something.

5. You ate something good.

6. You had a friend.

7. You felt energetic.

□ *Sight*
□ *Smell*
□ *Touch*
□ *Color*
□ *Tone*
□ *External Motion*
□ *Emotion*
□ *Loudness*
□ *Body Position*
□ *Sound*
□ *Weight*
□ *Personal Motion*

Can you recall a time when:

8. Somebody was waiting for you.

9. You drove fast.

10. You saw something you liked.

11. You acquired something good.

☐ *Sight*
☐ *Smell*
☐ *Touch*
☐ *Color*
☐ *Tone*
☐ *External Motion*
☐ *Emotion*
☐ *Loudness*
☐ *Body Position*
☐ *Sound*
☐ *Weight*
☐ *Personal Motion*

12. You threw away something bad.

13. You kissed somebody you liked.

14. You laughed at a joke.

15. You received money.

16. You felt young.

17. You liked life.

18. You played a game.

19. You bested something dangerous.

20. You acquired an animal.

21. Somebody thought you were important.

Can you recall a time when:

22. You chased something bad.

23. You were enthusiastic.

24. You owned something.

25. You enjoyed life.

26. You went fast.

27. You enjoyed a good loaf.

28. You felt strong.

29. Somebody you disliked departed.

30. Somebody helped you.

31. You gathered something good.

32. You measured something.

33. You took a pleasant journey.

34. You turned on a light.

35. You heard some good music.

☐ *Sight*
☐ *Smell*
☐ *Touch*
☐ *Color*
☐ *Tone*
☐ *External Motion*
☐ *Emotion*
☐ *Loudness*
☐ *Body Position*
☐ *Sound*
☐ *Weight*
☐ *Personal Motion*

Can you recall a time when:

36. You controlled something.

37. You destroyed something.

38. You mastered something.

39. You were lucky.

□ *Sight*
□ *Smell*
□ *Touch*
□ *Color*
□ *Tone*
□ *External Motion*
□ *Emotion*
□ *Loudness*
□ *Body Position*
□ *Sound*
□ *Weight*
□ *Personal Motion*

40. You felt peaceful.

41. You saw a pretty scene.

42. You poured something good.

43. You acquired something that was scarce.

44. You made an enemy scream.

45. You had a pleasant seat.

46. You handled something well (actual physical handling).

47. You moved something.

48. You watched something fast.

Can you recall a time when:

49. You were together with friends.

50. You occupied a good space.

51. Somebody loved you.

52. You enjoyed somebody.

53. You invented something.

54. You harnessed some energy.

55. You killed a bug.

56. You pocketed something.

57. You made progress.

58. You walked.

59. You saved something.

60. You stopped a machine.

61. You started a machine.

62. You had a good sleep.

□ *Sight*
□ *Smell*
□ *Touch*
□ *Color*
□ *Tone*
□ *External Motion*
□ *Emotion*
□ *Loudness*
□ *Body Position*
□ *Sound*
□ *Weight*
□ *Personal Motion*

Can you recall a time when:

63. You stopped a thief.

64. You stood under something.

65. You started a fire.

66. You went upstairs.

☐ *Sight*
☐ *Smell*
☐ *Touch*
☐ *Color*
☐ *Tone*
☐ *External Motion*
☐ *Emotion*
☐ *Loudness*
☐ *Body Position*
☐ *Sound*
☐ *Weight*
☐ *Personal Motion*

67. You were warm.

68. You went riding.

69. You were adroit.

70. You swam.

71. You stood your ground.

72. You lived well.

73. You were respected.

74. You won a race.

75. You ate well.

TIME ORIENTATION

This list is intended to aid your general sense of time as applied to periods in your life. Everyone has a full recording of everything that happened to him during his life. It may be that he cannot immediately recall certain periods. These periods are said to be occluded. Working with these lists in general, such occluded periods will gradually disappear when one's life is in recall—to the betterment of his mental and physical well-being and his perception of his present time environment.

In Dianetics, it is considered that everyone has a "time track." Everything which an individual has perceived throughout his life is recorded on this time track from the beginning to the end. It is dangerous to have occlusions since the data in the occluded area becomes compulsive and causes less than optimum conduct. This list is intended to straighten out the track in general. Do not be dismayed if you cannot recall the actual instant of the memory. Get the memory first. If you can answer the remaining questions, that is all to the good.

Can you recall an incident which happened:

1. A long time ago. (the year? the month? the date? the hour?)

2. Yesterday. (the hour? the date?)

3. Last month. (position of the Sun?)

□ *Sight*
□ *Smell*
□ *Touch*
□ *Color*
□ *Tone*
□ *External Motion*
□ *Emotion*
□ *Loudness*
□ *Body Position*
□ *Sound*
□ *Weight*
□ *Personal Motion*

4. When you were very small. (clothes people wore? position of the Sun?)

5. When you were half your present size. (the sizes of others at that time?)

6. When you were a third your present weight. (position of the Sun?)

7. When your mother looked younger. (her clothes? position of the Sun?)

8. When you felt agile. (the year? the hour?)

9. Last Christmas. (time of day?)

10. Your fifth Christmas. (clothing of others?)

Can you recall an incident which happened:

11. Your eighth birthday. (furniture?)

12. A birthday. (the appearance of others? year? position of the Sun?)

13. This day last year. (the house you lived in? the date? season?)

14. At noon today.

15. At a banquet. (clothing of people present?)

16. At a marriage. (year? season?)

17. At a birth. (season?)

18. On a date with someone. (hairdo?)

19. About a clock. (position of the Sun?)

20. About a wristwatch. (motion of second hand?)

21. With an animal. (when it was smaller?)

☐ *Sight*
☐ *Smell*
☐ *Touch*
☐ *Color*
☐ *Tone*
☐ *External Motion*
☐ *Emotion*
☐ *Loudness*
☐ *Body Position*
☐ *Sound*
☐ *Weight*
☐ *Personal Motion*

Can you recall incidents which compare:

1. Clothing today and clothing when you were small.

2. Hairdo today and hairdo when you were in your teens.

3. Something which is now old when it was new.

□ *Sight*
□ *Smell*
□ *Touch*
□ *Color*
□ *Tone*
□ *External Motion*
□ *Emotion*
□ *Loudness*
□ *Body Position*
□ *Sound*
□ *Weight*
□ *Personal Motion*

4. Something which was small which is now big.

5. Something which is now old when it was young.

6. The way the Sun shines in the morning and in the afternoon.

7. Winter with summer.

8. Spring with winter.

9. Fall with spring.

10. Sunrise with sunset.

11. A morning shadow and an evening shadow.

Can you recall incidents which compare:

12. Clothing now old when it was new.

13. A house now standing where no house was.

14. An open space which is now cut up.

15. A long time and a short time.

16. A cigarette when it was lighted and when it was put out.

17. The beginning and the end of a race.

18. Bedtime and getting up.

19. School in the morning and getting out in the afternoon.

20. Your size now and when you were little.

21. A cloudy day and a sunshiny day.

22. Stormy weather and rainy weather.

□ *Sight*
□ *Smell*
□ *Touch*
□ *Color*
□ *Tone*
□ *External Motion*
□ *Emotion*
□ *Loudness*
□ *Body Position*
□ *Sound*
□ *Weight*
□ *Personal Motion*

Can you recall incidents which compare:

23. Something hot and when it got cold.

24. Something young and something old.

25. A fast heartbeat and a slow heartbeat.

26. When you were overheated and when you were chilly.

□ *Sight*
□ *Smell*
□ *Touch*
□ *Color*
□ *Tone*
□ *External Motion*
□ *Emotion*
□ *Loudness*
□ *Body Position*
□ *Sound*
□ *Weight*
□ *Personal Motion*

27. When you had lots of room and when you had little room.

28. When the light was bright and when it was dim.

29. When a fire burned bright and when it died down.

30. An object half-built and when it was started.

31. The same person when he was big with when he was small.

32. When you felt little and when you felt grown up.

Can you recall incidents which compare:

33. Yesterday morning with this morning.

34. A complete calendar and when it had its leaves torn off.

35. A stopped clock and a running clock.

36. The Sun's motion and the Moon's motion.

37. When you felt tired and when you felt energetic.

38. Cars then with cars now.

39. When you started this list and this question.

☐ *Sight*
☐ *Smell*
☐ *Touch*
☐ *Color*
☐ *Tone*
☐ *External Motion*
☐ *Emotion*
☐ *Loudness*
☐ *Body Position*
☐ *Sound*
☐ *Weight*
☐ *Personal Motion*

ORIENTATION OF SENSES

This list is arranged especially to call your attention to the existence of many of the channels by which you perceive yourself and the physical universe about you. While each of the questions listed pertains to a specific sense channel, such as "Sight" or "Sound," the disk could still be used. For what is required are specific moments when you were using various senses and any specific moment includes many other sense messages than the one which is called for. Therefore, use the disk as in any other questions and after you have recalled a specific incident called for in the question, then try recalling it with specific attention to that sense which happens to be uppermost on the disk at that time.

TIME SENSE

Anyone has a sense of *time*. This sense is apt to become aberrated. The existence of clocks at every hand seems to tell us that we need mechanical assistance in knowing what time it is. The first person that had an aberrated or deranged time sense made the first clock desirable—but only for him. Clocks and calendars are artificial symbols representing time which is an actual commodity and which can be sensed directly by the individual. This section and almost every other section in these lists rehabilitate the sense of time. Time in most people's minds is confused with space. The words which describe time are also the words which describe space, which shows that Man has an indifferent attention for his time sense. The organism measures time in many ways, but mostly in terms of motion and growth or decay. Change is the most striking symbol of time passage. But there is a direct sense of time which everyone has, although it may be occluded by a society which—using clocks and calendars—seems to invalidate the fact that it exists. You should have no confusion of any kind about time.

Can you recall a time when:

□ *Sight*
□ *Smell*
□ *Touch*
□ *Color*
□ *Tone*
□ *External Motion*
□ *Emotion*
□ *Loudness*
□ *Body Position*
□ *Sound*
□ *Weight*
□ *Personal Motion*

1. It was very late.

2. You were early.

3. You had to wait.

4. You had to stand for some time supporting a weight.

5. You went very fast.

Can you recall a time when:

6. You covered a great deal of space.

7. You used a lot of time (when you really did, not when somebody said you did).

8. An object ran down (not a clock).

9. A long length of space.

10. A short length of space.

11. An object moving.

12. An animal moving.

13. A clock hand moving.

14. A round object.

15. An object near an object.

16. A lightning bolt.

17. Breaking a watch. (did time stop?)

18. A good time.

19. You were too late.

20. Somebody lived too long.

□ *Sight*
□ *Smell*
□ *Touch*
□ *Color*
□ *Tone*
□ *External Motion*
□ *Emotion*
□ *Loudness*
□ *Body Position*
□ *Sound*
□ *Weight*
□ *Personal Motion*

(Additional time questions are in the first half of List 2.)

SIGHT

There are several portions of the sense channel called *sight*. Light waves, coming from the Sun, Moon, stars or artificial sources, reflect from objects and the light waves enter the eyes and are recorded for present time action or as memory for future reference. Light sources are also recorded. This is the sense perception called sight. It has subdivisions.

First of these might be considered to be *motion*, wherein sight depends upon a timespan to record a continuously changing picture. While one may see motion in present time, various aberrations of sight may cause him to recall only still pictures. Nevertheless, all the motions are still recorded and can be recalled as moving pictures. In this way all other senses have a dependence upon time in order to bring in the message of motion, since motion is also recorded by the other perceptions.

More particularly, part of sight is *color perception*. There are people who are colorblind in present time—that is to say, they can see color but are unable to perceive differences of shading. There are people who may see color in present time but, in trying to recall what they have seen, recall only in black and white. This would be recall colorblindness. The color is fully deleted. It is an aberration easily remedied, when one recalls things he has seen in color as black and white or as still pictures.

Another part of sight is *depth perception*. Depth perception is observed in two ways. One is by seeing the difference in size of objects and so having a conception of the fact that one is further back than another or that the object itself is at a distance. And the other is a "stereoscopic" effect occasioned by the fact that one has two eyes. Each eye sees a little bit around the object and so true depth perception is possible. Still one may have two eyes and not have depth perception in present time observation. Additionally, one may see perfectly well with depth perception in present time and yet, in recall, see pictures flat and without depth perception. This lack of depth perception is again remediable.

An individual who could not perceive motion in present time and who additionally could not perceive color or depth would be a very bad risk as a driver—almost as bad as that individual who cannot recall what he has seen or, if he can recall it, cannot do so with depth perception, full color and motion. This part of this list is devoted to giving you a better insight into sight. All these perceptics are exercised over and over by these lists in general. If you cannot immediately see in recall what you have looked at some other time, simply try to get a concept of how things looked at specific times.

Can you recall a sight which was:

1. Very bright.

□ Sight
□ Smell
2. Dark.
□ Touch
□ Color
3. Green.
□ Tone
□ External
   Motion
4. Vast.
□ Emotion
□ Loudness
□ Body
5. Moving.
   Position
□ Sound
□ Weight
6. Flat.
□ Personal
   Motion

7. Deep.

Can you recall a sight which was:

8. Colorful.

9. Swift.

10. Slow.

11. Pleasant.

☐ *Sight*
☐ *Smell*
☐ *Touch*
☐ *Color*
☐ *Tone*
☐ *External Motion*
☐ *Emotion*
☐ *Loudness*
☐ *Body Position*
☐ *Sound*
☐ *Weight*
☐ *Personal Motion*

12. Desirable.

13. Pretty.

14. Rare.

15. Remarkable.

16. Confused.

17. Mysterious.

18. Lazy.

19. Warm.

20. Cheerful.

21. Nearly invisible.

Can you recall a sight which was:

22. Blurred.

23. Sharply defined.

24. Lovable.

25. Passionate.

26. Joyful.

27. Very real. (Something you can really recall well with sight.)

□ *Sight*
□ *Smell*
□ *Touch*
□ *Color*
□ *Tone*
□ *External Motion*
□ *Emotion*
□ *Loudness*
□ *Body Position*
□ *Sound*
□ *Weight*
□ *Personal Motion*

RELATIVE SIZES

The recognition of one's size in relationship to the scene in which he finds himself and the objects and organisms of that scene is, in itself, a sense message. It is particularly trying on children and undoubtedly was on you, when you were a child, to be surrounded with objects which were so large. When one is actually getting a good recall on a childhood incident, he is quite often startled to see how big things appeared to him and how large were those giants, the adults, with which he was surrounded. The feeling of being small in the vicinity of large objects sometimes produces the feeling of inadequacy. It is even said that people who are smaller than the average feel less secure in their environment. This evidently stems from the fact that their grown-up size has not reached the average and thus the feeling of smallness and inadequacy during childhood is in constant restimulation. It is not because the person, though smaller, is really inadequate. In such a way, people who are taller than the average become aware of the fact, mostly because people smaller than themselves find ways and means of nullifying them because of their size. The perception of *relative size* is therefore an important perception to rehabilitate. And a person who is larger than others on the average would do well to change the reading disk with which he is working these questions so that the word "Loudness" on the disk is marked out and "Relative Size" is substituted.

Can you recall a time when:

1. You were bigger than an animal.

2. You were smaller than an object.

3. You were bigger than a person.

Can you recall a time when:

4. You were smaller than a person.

5. Things looked little to you.

6. Things looked big to you.

7. You were in a vast space.

8. You looked at the stars.

9. You were dwarfed by an object.

10. You saw a giant.

11. Somebody waited on you.

12. You scared somebody.

13. You chased somebody.

14. You licked a larger boy.

15. Furniture was too small for you.

16. A bed was too small for you.

17. A bed was too big for you.

☐ *Sight*
☐ *Smell*
☐ *Touch*
☐ *Color*
☐ *Tone*
☐ *External Motion*
☐ *Emotion*
☐ *Loudness*
☐ *Body Position*
☐ *Sound*
☐ *Weight*
☐ *Personal Motion*

Can you recall a time when:

18. A hat didn't fit.

19. You had to be polite.

20. You bullied somebody.

21. Your clothes were too large.

22. Your clothes were too small.

☐ *Sight*

☐ *Smell*

☐ *Touch*   **23. The vehicle was too large.**

☐ *Color*

☐ *Tone*

☐ *External*   **24. The vehicle was too small.**
   Motion

☐ *Emotion*

☐ *Loudness*   **25. A space was too big.**

☐ *Body*
   Position

☐ *Sound*   **26. A table was too big.**

☐ *Weight*

☐ *Personal*   **27. Your arm was too big.**
   Motion

28. A cook was small.

29. You could reach something above you.

30. A ball was too small.

31. A daughter was smaller.

32. A desk was too small.

Can you recall:

33. A big fork.

34. A small kettle.

35. A small hill.

36. A small fish.

37. A little flower.

38. A small doctor.

39. A tiny dog.

40. A small man.

41. A little child.

42. A small cat.

43. A little house.

44. A small machine.

45. Short legs.

46. A small face.

47. A small place.

□ *Sight*
□ *Smell*
□ *Touch*
□ *Color*
□ *Tone*
□ *External Motion*
□ *Emotion*
□ *Loudness*
□ *Body Position*
□ *Sound*
□ *Weight*
□ *Personal Motion*

Sound

Sound consists of the perception of waves emanating from moving objects. An object moves, rapidly or slowly, and sets into vibration the air in its vicinity which pulses. When these pulses strike the eardrum, they set into motion the individual's sound-recording mechanism and the sound is registered. Sound is absent in a vacuum and is actually merely a force wave. Sound in too great a volume or too discordant can be physically painful, just as light in too great a quantity can hurt the eyes. However, the amount of nervousness occasioned by sound, as by light, is mainly an aberration and it is not warranted, since the sound itself is not ordinarily damaging and there are few incidents in anyone's life when a sound has had enough physical force to be physically damaging. Apprehension and anxiety about the physical universe and other persons can, however, cause the individual to be nervous about sound, as it is one of the most reliable warning mechanisms. But starting at every sound in a civilized environment, being afraid of voices of others, or even traffic noises, is foolish, since men rarely live a tooth and claw existence which warrants such attention. As sound becomes intermingled with past pain, the individual mistakes the moment and time he is hearing the sound and so may associate it, as he may with other perceptics, with past pain. These lists permit an individual to rehabilitate his skill in telling the difference between one time and another or one situation and another.

Sound has several parts. The first is *pitch*. This is the number of vibrations per unit of time of any object from which sound is coming. The second is *quality* or *tone*, which is simply the difference between a jagged or ragged sound wave and a smooth sound wave, as in a musical note. The third is *volume*, which merely means the force of the sound wave, its loudness or quietness.

Rhythm is actually a part of the time sense, but is also the ability to tell the spaces between sound waves which are pulsing regularly, as in the beating of a drum.

Many people have what is called *extended hearing*—which is to say, they have too high an alertness to sounds. This accompanies, quite ordinarily, a general fear of the environment or the people in it. There is also *deafness* by which the individual simply shuts out sounds. Some deafness is, of course, occasioned by entirely mechanical trouble with the recording mechanism. But most deafness, particularly when partial, is "psychosomatic," or caused by mental aberration. The individual may or may not be able, at first, to recall what he has heard—and which has been recorded in the past—when he remembers it. In other words, he does not get a sound when he remembers that he heard a sound. This is an occlusion of sound recordings. Recalling a sound by hearing it again is called "sonic," in Dianetics, and is a desirable circumstance which can be returned to the individual.

It is interesting to note that there is also a *depth perception* in sound. A person having two ears gets a "stereophonic" effect on sources of sound so that he can tell how far they are from him and where they are located in relationship to him.

Can you recall a time when you heard:

1. A gentle wind.

2. A quiet voice.

3. A pleasant sound.

4. A pleasant voice.

☐ Sight
☐ Smell
☐ Touch
☐ Color
☐ Tone
☐ External Motion
☐ Emotion
☐ Loudness
☐ Body Position
☐ Sound
☐ Weight
☐ Personal Motion

Can you recall a time when you heard:

5. A breeze.

6. A dog whining.

7. A bell.

8. A cheerful voice.

□ *Sight*
□ *Smell*
□ *Touch*
□ *Color*
□ *Tone*
□ *External Motion*
□ *Emotion*
□ *Loudness*
□ *Body Position*
□ *Sound*
□ *Weight*
□ *Personal Motion*

9. A musical instrument.

10. A door close.

11. Water running.

12. Liquid coming from a bottle.

13. Good food frying.

14. A ball rolling.

15. A wheel singing.

16. A car starting.

17. A child laughing.

Can you recall a time when you heard:

18. A ball bouncing.

19. A sewing machine running.

20. A cat mewing.

21. A pen writing.

☐ *Sight*
☐ *Smell*
☐ *Touch*
☐ *Color*
☐ *Tone*
☐ *External Motion*
☐ *Emotion*
☐ *Loudness*
☐ *Body Position*
☐ *Sound*
☐ *Weight*
☐ *Personal Motion*

22. A child running.

23. A book page turning.

24. A newspaper being opened.

25. A kiss.

26. A stimulating sound.

27. A smooth sound.

28. A rhythmic sound.

29. A happy sound.

30. A rubbing sound.

Can you recall a time when you heard:

31. An enthusiastic sound.

32. A sigh.

33. An eager voice.

34. A revelry.

☐ *Sight*
☐ *Smell*   **35. A band.**
☐ *Touch*
☐ *Color*
☐ *Tone*   **36. A silky sound.**
☐ *External
   Motion*
☐ *Emotion*
☐ *Loudness* **37. Restful water.**
☐ *Body
   Position*
☐ *Sound*   **38. A sound in a big place.**
☐ *Weight*
☐ *Personal
   Motion*   **39. A wanted sound.**

40. An endearing sound.

41. A domestic sound.

42. A busy sound.

43. A pleasant noise.

Can you recall a time when you heard:

44. A far-off sound.

45. A nearby sound.

46. A number of sounds jumbled together.

47. A safe sound.

48. A sound that is very real to you.

□ *Sight*
□ *Smell*
□ *Touch*
□ *Color*
□ *Tone*
□ *External Motion*
□ *Emotion*
□ *Loudness*
□ *Body Position*
□ *Sound*
□ *Weight*
□ *Personal Motion*

OLFACTORY

The sense of *smell* is evidently activated by small particles escaping from the object, which is thus sensed traveling through space and meeting the nerves. When one comes to think of it, this seems rather unpleasant at times. But there are also many very pleasant smells.

The sense of smell has four subdivisions, which are mainly categories of the type of odor.

Taste is usually considered to be a part of the sense of smell.

Can you recall a time when you smelled the following:

□ *Sight*
□ *Smell*
□ *Touch*
□ *Color*
□ *Tone*
□ *External Motion*
□ *Emotion*
□ *Loudness*
□ *Body Position*
□ *Sound*
□ *Weight*
□ *Personal Motion*

1. Something sweet.

2. Something sharp.

3. Something oily.

4. Something pungent.

5. Something desirable.

6. Something burned.

7. Something stimulating.

8. Something cheerful.

9. A good person.

Can you recall a time when you smelled the following:

10. A happy person.

11. A warm person.

12. A friendly animal.

13. A pleasant leaf.

14. Cut grass.

15. Something passionate.

16. Something you wanted.

17. Something you threw away.

18. A bird.

19. Something exciting.

20. Something desirable.

21. A child.

22. Face powder.

23. Perfume.

☐ *Sight*
☐ *Smell*
☐ *Touch*
☐ *Color*
☐ *Tone*
☐ *External Motion*
☐ *Emotion*
☐ *Loudness*
☐ *Body Position*
☐ *Sound*
☐ *Weight*
☐ *Personal Motion*

Can you recall a time when you smelled the following:

24. Lipstick.

25. Leather.

26. Pipe smoke.

27. Sweat.

28. Wool.

□ *Sight*
□ *Smell*
□ *Touch*
□ *Color*
□ *Tone*
□ *External Motion*
□ *Emotion*
□ *Loudness*
□ *Body Position*
□ *Sound*
□ *Weight*
□ *Personal Motion*

29. Clean sheets.

30. Fresh air.

31. A bouquet.

32. Money.

33. Paper.

34. Furniture.

35. A beautiful morning.

36. A party.

37. A pleasant odor that is very real to you.

Can you recall a time when you tasted the following:

1. Soup.

2. Eggs.

3. Bread.

4. Biscuits.

5. Coffee.

☐ *Sight*
☐ *Smell*
☐ *Touch*

6. Tea.

☐ *Color*
☐ *Tone*
☐ *External*
   Motion

7. Milk.

☐ *Emotion*
☐ *Loudness*

8. Cereal.

☐ *Body*
   Position
☐ *Sound*

9. Dumplings.

☐ *Weight*
☐ *Personal*
   Motion

10. Fish.

11. Beef.

12. Chicken.

13. A steak.

14. Duck.

Can you recall a time when you tasted the following:

15. Stuffing.

16. Cheese.

17. A fillet.

18. Potatoes.

□ *Sight*
□ *Smell*
□ *Touch*
□ *Color*
□ *Tone*
□ *External Motion*
□ *Emotion*
□ *Loudness*
□ *Body Position*
□ *Sound*
□ *Weight*
□ *Personal Motion*

19. Watermelon.

20. A cocktail.

21. Liquor.

22. A hot sandwich.

23. Jelly.

24. Ice cream.

25. Pudding.

26. Candy.

27. Pickles.

28. Punch.

Can you recall a time when you tasted the following:

29. A vegetable.

30. An apple.

31. An orange.

32. A fruit.

33. Cake.

34. Something you really thought was well cooked.

35. Something you like to eat raw.

36. A cookie.

37. A cracker.

38. Meat.

39. Something cold.

40. Something warm.

41. Your favorite dish.

☐ *Sight*
☐ *Smell*
☐ *Touch*
☐ *Color*
☐ *Tone*
☐ *External Motion*
☐ *Emotion*
☐ *Loudness*
☐ *Body Position*
☐ *Sound*
☐ *Weight*
☐ *Personal Motion*

Can you recall a time when you tasted the following:

42. Something in a swanky place.

43. Something at a party.

44. Something in the open.

45. Something on a holiday.

☐ *Sight*
☐ *Smell*
☐ *Touch*
☐ *Color*
☐ *Tone*
☐ *External Motion*
☐ *Emotion*
☐ *Loudness*
☐ *Body Position*
☐ *Sound*
☐ *Weight*
☐ *Personal Motion*

46. Something when you were very hungry.

47. Something which was rare.

48. Something which made you feel good.

49. Something for which you were grateful.

50. Something you had waited for, for a long time.

51. Something you had not been able to get.

52. Something you stole.

Touch

The sense of *touch* is that communication channel which informs the central control system of the body whenever some portion of the body is in contact with the material universe, other organisms or the organism itself. Probably the sense of touch is the oldest sense in the terms of the central nervous system. It has four subdivisions. The first of these is *pressure*, the second is *friction*, the third is *heat* or *cold* and the last is *oiliness*.

Just as an individual can be hard of hearing or have bad eyesight, so can his sense of touch be dulled or even almost absent. This condition is known as *anesthesia*. Just as in any other perceptic, the sense of touch can be pleasurable, unpleasant or painful. When an individual has been considerably harmed, as in accidents, illness or injury, he tends to cut communication with the physical universe and other organisms, just as he cuts communication by getting bad eyesight, becoming hard of hearing, etc. Not only can the sense of touch be dulled in some people, but it can be too sensitive in others—who have this sense channel aberrated—until it seeks to contact danger more avidly than danger exists. One of the manifestations of the aberrated sense of touch is too high a sensitivity to sexual contact, rendering it painful or anxious, or a dulling of this contact so that sensation can be nearly absent. A sense of touch is very important. It is partially responsible for pleasure, as in sex, and is to a large measure responsible for the sensation we know as physical pain. The sense of touch extends from the central nervous system to the skin surface and as such is intimately connected and most basically in contact with the physical universe. Sight and sound and the olfactory systems contact things usually at a distance, whereas touch is alert only to the closest proximity of actual contact. Touch is partially responsible for the pleasure taken in food and crosses, to this extent, the sense of taste.

As a demonstration of how poorly the sense of touch serves many people, try laying your hand in a friendly fashion on the shoulder of someone. All too many people will dodge or shrink away from the contact. An aberrated sense of touch is partially responsible for a dislike of food as well as impotency and antipathy for the sexual act. The rehabilitation of the sense of touch goes a long way toward rehabilitating one's confidence in one's environment and considerably enhances survival by making it possible for the individual to obtain pleasure, where before there might only have been distaste.

Can you recall an incident when you felt (touched):

☐ *Sight*
☐ *Smell*
☐ *Touch*
☐ *Color*
☐ *Tone*
☐ *External Motion*
☐ *Emotion*
☐ *Loudness*
☐ *Body Position*
☐ *Sound*
☐ *Weight*
☐ *Personal Motion*

1. The pressure on your feet while you stood.

2. A fork.

3. A greasy surface.

4. The pressure of a movie seat.

5. A steering wheel.

6. A cat.

7. Another person.

8. Cool clothing.

9. Your hair.

10. A child.

Can you recall an incident when you felt (touched):

11. Something you admired.

12. Something new.

13. An arm.

14. A ball.

15. An easy chair.

16. A collar.

17. A poker.

18. A musical instrument.

19. Something comfortable.

20. Something which gave you confidence.

21. Something bright.

22. A desk.

23. A girl.

24. A boy.

25. A fish.

26. A doll.

☐ *Sight*
☐ *Smell*
☐ *Touch*
☐ *Color*
☐ *Tone*
☐ *External
  Motion*
☐ *Emotion*
☐ *Loudness*
☐ *Body
  Position*
☐ *Sound*
☐ *Weight*
☐ *Personal
  Motion*

Can you recall an incident when you felt (touched):

27. Silk.

28. Velvet.

29. Your ear.

30. Your body.

31. Something which made you feel enthusiastic.

□ *Sight*
□ *Smell*
□ *Touch*
□ *Color*
□ *Tone*
□ *External Motion*
□ *Emotion*
□ *Loudness*
□ *Body Position*
□ *Sound*
□ *Weight*
□ *Personal Motion*

32. Something which delighted you.

33. Something you desired eagerly.

34. Someone who was faithful.

35. A happy child.

36. A generous hand.

37. A good machine.

38. A pleasant letter.

39. A newspaper containing good news.

40. A telephone when you received good news.

41. A hat.

Can you recall an incident when you felt (touched):

42. A dear face.

43. A stair banister.

44. A kind object.

45. A moving object.

46. An object you loved.

47. An enemy being hurt.

48. A polite person.

49. Something pretty.

50. Something which made you rejoice.

51. A food you liked.

52. Something you believed in.

53. Something you liked to stroke.

54. A strong person.

55. A little person.

☐ *Sight*
☐ *Smell*
☐ *Touch*
☐ *Color*
☐ *Tone*
☐ *External Motion*
☐ *Emotion*
☐ *Loudness*
☐ *Body Position*
☐ *Sound*
☐ *Weight*
☐ *Personal Motion*

Can you recall an incident when you felt (touched):

56. Water you enjoyed.

57. A shower.

58. An old person.

☐ *Sight*
☐ *Smell*
☐ *Touch*
☐ *Color*
☐ *Tone*
☐ *External Motion*
☐ *Emotion*
☐ *Loudness*
☐ *Body Position*
☐ *Sound*
☐ *Weight*
☐ *Personal Motion*

59. Something warm.

60. Something cold.

61. A wind.

62. A sleepy person.

63. A cool bed on a warm night.

64. Something which made you enthusiastic.

65. Something you touched this morning.

66. Something you are touching now.

PERSONAL EMOTION

There are many *emotions*. The principal ones are *happiness, boredom, antagonism, anger, covert hostility, fear, grief* and *apathy*. Other emotions are usually simply greater or lesser magnitude than the ones listed. Terror, for instance, is a volume of fear. Sadness is a small volume of grief. Dejection is a small part of apathy. Love is an intensity of happiness addressed in a certain direction. These emotions form a gradient scale which make up, in Dianetics, the emotion section of the Tone Scale. Happiness is the highest emotion and apathy is the lowest. A person can be chronically emotional along any level of this Tone Scale. An individual tends to move up or down this scale through these various listed emotions in the order of the second sentence.

Emotion monitors or regulates the endocrine system. The perceptions and the central nervous system call for certain emotional secretions to catalyze the body to meet the various situations in the environment. Emotion is one of the easiest things to aberrate. There are individuals who feel they must be perpetually sad even when their circumstances should make them happy. There are individuals who believe they have to be happy regardless of their environment and who yet are very miserable. Most people are not emotional, they are *mis-emotional*—in that they do not react to the situations in their environment with the emotion which would be most rational to display. The social order has confused rationality with emotionalism. Actually, a person who is fully rational would be most able to respond to the stimulus of his environment. Being rational does not mean being cold and calculating. An individual who is rationally happy can be counted upon to make the best calculations. Without free emotion, an individual cannot appreciate, as he should, the pleasant things in his environment.

Lack of appreciation for art or music comes about when the individual cannot be freely emotional. The person who feels he must be cold-blooded in order to be rational is what is called, in Dianetics, a "control case," and on examination will be found to be very far from as rational as he might be. People who cannot experience emotion because of their aberrations are ordinarily sick people. Well people can experience emotion.

Derangements in the endocrine system, such as the thyroid, the pancreas and other glands, come about because of aberrations concerning emotion. It has been conclusively tested and proven in Dianetics that function controls structure. To a man or a woman who is aberrated sexually, injections of hormones are of little or no avail in moving the mental aberrations which make injections ineffective. Removing emotional aberration rehabilitates the endocrine system so that the injections are usually not even necessary. When a person's emotional reaction becomes frozen, he can expect various physical difficulties such as ulcers, hypothyroid conditions, diabetes and other ills which are more or less directly traceable to the endocrine system.

Inhibited or excessive mis-emotionalism is one of the most destructive things which can occur in the human organism. A person who is so aberrated is unable to experience happiness and so enjoy life. His physical body will not thrive.

Can you recall an incident when:

1. Somebody was angry.

2. Somebody wanted something.

3. You desired something.

4. You were happy.

Can you recall an incident when:

5. You were pleased.

6. You won by being antagonistic.

7. You felt affectionate.

8. You admired something.

9. Something was amiable.

10. You were amused.

11. You approved of an object.

12. You were surprised by something pleasant.

□ *Sight*
□ *Smell*
□ *Touch*
□ *Color*
□ *Tone*
□ *External Motion*
□ *Emotion*
□ *Loudness*
□ *Body Position*
□ *Sound*
□ *Weight*
□ *Personal Motion*

13. You attacked something successfully.

14. You attacked someone.

15. You were "attached" to something.

16. You had to blush.

17. You felt bold.

Can you recall an incident when:

18. You couldn't be bothered.

19. You were energetic.

20. You found out you weren't clumsy.

21. You were satisfied.

□ *Sight*
□ *Smell*
□ *Touch*
□ *Color*
□ *Tone*
□ *External Motion*
□ *Emotion*
□ *Loudness*
□ *Body Position*
□ *Sound*
□ *Weight*
□ *Personal Motion*

22. You cared for somebody.

23. You were confident.

24. You influenced somebody.

25. You were glad to be idle.

26. Somebody was patient.

27. You enjoyed life.

28. You were joyful.

29. You laughed.

30. You were in love.

31. You received good news.

Can you recall an incident when:

32. You enjoyed the music.

33. You thought it was pretty.

34. You were satiated.

35. You were passionate.

36. You prevented something.

37. You produced something.

38. You were glad to avoid a quarrel.

39. You were glad to hurt somebody.

40. You rejoiced.

41. You felt very safe.

42. You screamed with laughter.

43. You enjoyed the silence.

44. You got to go to bed.

45. You found it was a beautiful day.

☐ *Sight*
☐ *Smell*
☐ *Touch*
☐ *Color*
☐ *Tone*
☐ *External Motion*
☐ *Emotion*
☐ *Loudness*
☐ *Body Position*
☐ *Sound*
☐ *Weight*
☐ *Personal Motion*

Can you recall an incident when:

46. You won the struggle.

47. You subdued a person.

48. You conquered something.

49. You obtained what you wanted.

□ *Sight*
□ *Smell*
□ *Touch*
□ *Color*
□ *Tone*
□ *External Motion*
□ *Emotion*
□ *Loudness*
□ *Body Position*
□ *Sound*
□ *Weight*
□ *Personal Motion*

50. You surprised somebody.

51. You contributed.

52. You were permitted to handle something.

53. You were glad you didn't have to be sorry.

54. You found the anxiety was for nothing.

55. You discovered your suspicions were unfounded.

56. You finally got rid of it.

57. You stopped somebody from being terrified.

Can you recall an incident when:

58. You were happy.

59. Somebody understood you.

60. Somebody listened to you respectfully.

61. You felt energetic.

62. You were vigorous.

63. You knew it was well done.

64. You didn't have to wait anymore.

65. You liked to watch.

66. You stopped somebody from weeping.

67. You wandered at will.

68. You felt free.

69. You helped somebody.

70. You felt young.

71. You won.

☐ *Sight*
☐ *Smell*
☐ *Touch*
☐ *Color*
☐ *Tone*
☐ *External Motion*
☐ *Emotion*
☐ *Loudness*
☐ *Body Position*
☐ *Sound*
☐ *Weight*
☐ *Personal Motion*

Can you recall an incident when:

72. You were glad to be together.

73. You were glad to leave.

74. You liked emotion.

75. You enjoyed moving.

□ *Sight*
□ *Smell*
□ *Touch*
□ *Color*
□ *Tone*
□ *External*
Motion
□ *Emotion*
□ *Loudness*
□ *Body*
Position
□ *Sound*
□ *Weight*
□ *Personal*
Motion

76. The motion gave you joy.

77. You caught sight of something you had been waiting for.

78. You received a present you liked.

79. You found something out.

80. You pushed something away.

81. You pulled something to you.

82. You produced something.

83. You were proud of it.

84. You raised something high.

Can you recall an incident when:

85. You prevailed.

86. You harnessed some energy.

87. You made the time pleasant.

88. You were glad to be with a friend.

89. You made something obey.

90. You were happy to give offense.

91. You realized your luck was good.

92. You overcame antagonism.

93. You found it was fun to leap.

94. You got out of work.

95. You didn't have to sit there anymore.

96. You realized it was the last day of school.

97. You were happy it was real.

☐ *Sight*
☐ *Smell*
☐ *Touch*
☐ *Color*
☐ *Tone*
☐ *External Motion*
☐ *Emotion*
☐ *Loudness*
☐ *Body Position*
☐ *Sound*
☐ *Weight*
☐ *Personal Motion*

Can you recall an incident when:

98. You felt virtuous.

99. You knew you had shown courage.

100. Your desire was gratified.

101. You succeeded in your deception.

□ *Sight*
□ *Smell*
□ *Touch*
□ *Color*
□ *Tone*
□ *External
Motion*
□ *Emotion*
□ *Loudness*
□ *Body
Position*
□ *Sound*
□ *Weight*
□ *Personal
Motion*

102. You conquered dejection.

103. You were glad it was over.

104. You waited eagerly.

105. You dispersed them.

106. You could tell the difference.

107. Your parent was proud of you.

108. Somebody was faithful to you.

109. You escaped.

110. You found you had hidden without cause.

Can you recall an incident when:

111. You frightened somebody.

112. You overcame conservatism.

113. You discovered a friend.

114. You were friendly.

115. You did something that was forbidden and got away with it.

☐ *Sight*
☐ *Smell*
☐ *Touch*
☐ *Color*
☐ *Tone*
☐ *External Motion*
☐ *Emotion*
☐ *Loudness*
☐ *Body Position*
☐ *Sound*
☐ *Weight*
☐ *Personal Motion*

116. You gave somebody the gate.

117. You healed something.

118. You acquired a pet.

119. It was a relief.

120. You found you weren't hurt.

121. You received a pleasant call.

122. Your income was increased.

123. You found you had influence.

Can you recall an incident when:

124. You were ambitious.

125. You succeeded.

126. You found you didn't want it after all.

127. You conquered being poor.

□ *Sight*
□ *Smell*
□ *Touch*
□ *Color*
□ *Tone*
□ *External Motion*
□ *Emotion*
□ *Loudness*
□ *Body Position*
□ *Sound*
□ *Weight*
□ *Personal Motion*

128. Many were proud of you.

129. You were loved.

130. They rejoiced for you.

131. You were considered remarkable.

132. You kept a secret.

133. Someone believed in you.

134. You understood.

135. You showed your skill.

136. They liked you.

137. Somebody was happy.

Can you recall an incident when:

138. Someone appreciated you.

139. You felt you had done a good job.

140. A child loved you.

141. A friend needed you.

142. They laughed at your joke.

143. Everybody was surprised.

144. You were sought after.

145. You were invited.

146. Someone made you realize you were strong.

147. You were important.

148. You found yourself necessary.

149. It was worthwhile.

150. You knew you had given pleasure.

☐ *Sight*
☐ *Smell*
☐ *Touch*
☐ *Color*
☐ *Tone*
☐ *External Motion*
☐ *Emotion*
☐ *Loudness*
☐ *Body Position*
☐ *Sound*
☐ *Weight*
☐ *Personal Motion*

Can you recall an incident when:

151. You were well.

152. Someone was delighted with you.

153. You won the struggle.

154. You were believed.

□ *Sight*
□ *Smell*
□ *Touch*
□ *Color*
□ *Tone*
□ *External Motion*
□ *Emotion*
□ *Loudness*
□ *Body Position*
□ *Sound*
□ *Weight*
□ *Personal Motion*

155. You rescued somebody.

156. You discovered you weren't weak.

157. They stopped fighting you.

158. Somebody became afraid of you.

159. You made somebody successful.

160. You dispersed anxiety.

161. You were looked up to.

162. Somebody was glad you were there.

163. You conquered sorrow.

164. You were glad they were watching.

Can you recall an incident when:

**165. You could go and come as you
pleased.**

166. They gave you a chair.

167. You were rewarded.

168. You decided for yourself.

□ *Sight*
□ *Smell*

169. You found you were right.

□ *Touch*
□ *Color*
□ *Tone*

170. You enjoyed youth.

□ *External
Motion*
□ *Emotion*

171. You yelled for happiness.

□ *Loudness*
□ *Body
Position*

172. You received what you wanted.

□ *Sound*
□ *Weight*
□ *Personal
Motion*

173. They discovered you were valuable.

174. You gave great happiness.

175. You were glad you had done it.

176. You found you weren't vain after all.

177. You avoided them successfully.

Can you recall an incident when:

178. You became important.

179. You were no longer unhappy.

180. You got to go.

181. You conquered some energy.

□ *Sight*
□ *Smell*
□ *Touch*
□ *Color*
□ *Tone*
□ *External Motion*
□ *Emotion*
□ *Loudness*
□ *Body Position*
□ *Sound*
□ *Weight*
□ *Personal Motion*

182. You fixed it.

183. They found you had been wrongly suspected.

184. Your understanding was swift.

185. You discovered you didn't have to be ashamed.

186. You succeeded in your struggle.

187. You were glad to shake hands.

188. You enjoyed the kiss.

189. It was good to run.

190. You were able to retain it.

Can you recall an incident when:

191. You restored it.

192. You did not have to go to bed.

193. You averted ruin.

194. You found a refuge.

195. It was good not to have to regret it.

196. You were true to your purpose.

197. You had lots of time.

198. You got out.

199. Somebody was glad you wrote.

□ *Sight*
□ *Smell*
□ *Touch*
□ *Color*
□ *Tone*
□ *External Motion*
□ *Emotion*
□ *Loudness*
□ *Body Position*
□ *Sound*
□ *Weight*
□ *Personal Motion*

200. Your people appreciated you.

201. You grew up.

202. You could make all the noise you wanted.

203. It wasn't necessary to do anything.

Can you recall an incident when:

204. You obliged somebody.

205. It was a wonderful occasion.

206. You were glad you were in love.

207. You couldn't lose.

□ *Sight*
□ *Smell*
□ *Touch*
□ *Color*
□ *Tone*
□ *External Motion*
□ *Emotion*
□ *Loudness*
□ *Body Position*
□ *Sound*
□ *Weight*
□ *Personal Motion*

208. You got them enthusiastic.

209. You sold it.

210. They enjoyed your music.

211. You laughed last.

212. You found out you weren't lazy.

213. They discovered you weren't ignorant.

214. They wanted your influence.

215. You didn't have to hurry.

216. You illuminated something beautiful.

Can you recall an incident when:

217. You did the impossible.

218. You didn't have to worry about income.

219. You saw somebody come in that you liked.

220. You saw somebody leave that you disliked.

221. You felt fit.

222. Your fears were groundless.

223. It was all right to be excited.

224. You felt equal to anything.

225. It was a brilliant morning.

226. Life was full of zest.

227. They let you have enough.

228. The drink was welcome.

229. You were glad to eat.

☐ *Sight*
☐ *Smell*
☐ *Touch*
☐ *Color*
☐ *Tone*
☐ *External Motion*
☐ *Emotion*
☐ *Loudness*
☐ *Body Position*
☐ *Sound*
☐ *Weight*
☐ *Personal Motion*

Can you recall an incident when:

230. It was so good to hug someone.

231. You delivered the goods.

232. You were depended upon.

233. Nobody could deny you anything.

☐ *Sight*
☐ *Smell*
☐ *Touch*
☐ *Color*
☐ *Tone*
☐ *External Motion*
☐ *Emotion*
☐ *Loudness*
☐ *Body Position*
☐ *Sound*
☐ *Weight*
☐ *Personal Motion*

234. You found you hadn't been deceived.

235. You deserved it.

236. You crawled under the covers.

237. They let you continue.

238. You could be as contrary as you wanted.

239. The doctor was wrong.

240. Somebody cooked for you.

241. You had a nice house.

242. You found it was a pretty country.

Can you recall an incident when:

243. You discovered you didn't have to stay there.

244. You got a better title.

245. You found something valuable.

246. You could keep any company you wanted.

247. You discovered it wasn't too complicated.

248. They had confidence in you.

249. You helped them conquer something.

250. You could leave the classroom.

251. You didn't have to go there anymore.

252. Somebody came when you called.

253. You enjoyed a new car.

254. You got out of the cage.

255. They admitted you were clever.

☐ *Sight*
☐ *Smell*
☐ *Touch*
☐ *Color*
☐ *Tone*
☐ *External Motion*
☐ *Emotion*
☐ *Loudness*
☐ *Body Position*
☐ *Sound*
☐ *Weight*
☐ *Personal Motion*

Can you recall an incident when:

256. You found your hands were adroit.

257. You discovered you could run faster.

258. You discovered you didn't have to mind.

259. You found it wasn't in vain after all.

☐ *Sight*
☐ *Smell*
☐ *Touch*
☐ *Color*
☐ *Tone*
☐ *External Motion*
☐ *Emotion*
☐ *Loudness*
☐ *Body Position*
☐ *Sound*
☐ *Weight*
☐ *Personal Motion*

260. Hope paid off.

261. You had a right to think for yourself.

262. You found you didn't have to be disappointed.

263. You discovered how persistent you were.

264. You knew you could handle responsibility.

265. The world was all yours.

266. You were delighted.

267. You felt good this morning.

Oʀɢᴀɴɪᴄ Sᴇɴsᴀᴛɪᴏɴ

Organic sensation is that sense which tells the central nervous system the state of the various organs of the body. Don't be alarmed if you feel groggy for a while or if you yawn prodigiously. These manifestations are good and they will pass away if you recall a certain additional number of recollections on the same question that made you feel strange.

Can you recall a time when:

1. You felt yourself to be in good physical condition.

2. You enjoyed yourself physically.

□ *Sight*

3. You had just eaten something you liked.

□ *Smell*
□ *Touch*
□ *Color*

4. Your head felt good.

□ *Tone*
□ *External Motion*

5. Your back felt good.

□ *Emotion*
□ *Loudness*
□ *Body Position*

6. You felt very relieved.

□ *Sound*
□ *Weight*

7. You were excited.

□ *Personal Motion*

8. You felt very much alive.

9. You were proud of your body.

Can you recall a time when:

10. Your body was competent.

11. Your heart was beating calmly.

12. You didn't have a single ache or pain.

13. You felt refreshed.

☐ *Sight*
☐ *Smell*
☐ *Touch*
☐ *Color*
☐ *Tone*
☐ *External Motion*
☐ *Emotion*
☐ *Loudness*
☐ *Body Position*
☐ *Sound*
☐ *Weight*
☐ *Personal Motion*

14. Everybody was having a good time.

15. Both of you enjoyed it.

16. Your back felt strong.

17. You stood very straight.

18. You liked your position.

19. You got a new position.

20. You needed and got a cool drink of water.

21. Your head felt clear.

22. It was good to breathe fresh air.

Can you recall a time when:

23. You got it up.

24. You got it out.

25. You felt strong again.

26. You had eaten a good dinner.

□ *Sight*
□ *Smell*
□ *Touch*
□ *Color*
□ *Tone*
□ *External Motion*
□ *Emotion*
□ *Loudness*
□ *Body Position*
□ *Sound*
□ *Weight*
□ *Personal Motion*

27. You were enjoying it.

28. You did it with ease.

29. You poured something out.

30. You were tense with excitement.

31. You were relaxed.

32. Your chest felt good.

33. Your throat felt good.

34. Your eyes felt good.

35. You weren't aware of your breathing.

Can you recall a time when:

☐ *Sight*
☐ *Smell*
☐ *Touch*
☐ *Color*
☐ *Tone*
☐ *External Motion*
☐ *Emotion*
☐ *Loudness*
☐ *Body Position*
☐ *Sound*
☐ *Weight*
☐ *Personal Motion*

36. Your ears weren't ringing.

37. Your hands did something competent.

38. Your legs served you well.

39. Your feet felt good.

40. You knew you looked good.

M OTION P ERSONAL

Amongst the various perceptions is that of *personal motion.* This is awareness of change of position in space. Many other perceptions assist this awareness of motion of self. This perception is assisted by sight, the feel of wind, changes in body weight and by the observation of external environment. However, it is a perceptic in itself and in the following questions, your attention is called simply to the internal awareness of yourself in motion.

Can you recall a time when:

1. You were running.

2. You were walking.

3. You enjoyed a stroll.

4. You overcame something.

5. You threw something away you didn't want.

6. You won a tug of war.

7. You skipped rope.

8. You rode.

9. You did something successful in sports.

☐ *Sight*
☐ *Smell*
☐ *Touch*
☐ *Color*
☐ *Tone*
☐ *External Motion*
☐ *Emotion*
☐ *Loudness*
☐ *Body Position*
☐ *Sound*
☐ *Weight*
☐ *Personal Motion*

Can you recall a time when:

10. You lay down.

11. You stood up.

12. You turned around and around.

13. You jumped.

□ *Sight*
□ *Smell*
□ *Touch*
□ *Color*
□ *Tone*
□ *External Motion*
□ *Emotion*
□ *Loudness*
□ *Body Position*
□ *Sound*
□ *Weight*
□ *Personal Motion*

14. You stood on something that moved.

15. You leaped up.

16. You won a race.

17. You did something you were admired for physically.

18. You enjoyed moving.

19. You enjoyed standing still.

20. You pointed out something.

21. You showed yourself superior physically.

22. Your right hand did something skillful.

Can you recall a time when:

23. Your left hand did something skillful.

24. You tamed an animal.

25. You bested another person.

26. You did something physical you enjoyed.

☐ *Sight*
☐ *Smell*

27. You stepped up.

☐ *Touch*
☐ *Color*
☐ *Tone*

28. You held something close to you.

☐ *External Motion*
☐ *Emotion*
☐ *Loudness*

29. You threw something away you didn't want.

☐ *Body Position*
☐ *Sound*
☐ *Weight*

30. You felt lazy.

☐ *Personal Motion*

31. You turned the page of a book you enjoyed reading.

32. You dressed.

33. You got up when you wanted to.

34. You enjoyed wrestling with somebody.

Can you recall a time when:

35. You handled a complicated object successfully.

36. You drove well.

37. You carried some weight.

38. You gathered things together.

□ *Sight*
□ *Smell*
□ *Touch*
□ *Color*
□ *Tone*
□ *External Motion*
□ *Emotion*
□ *Loudness*
□ *Body Position*
□ *Sound*
□ *Weight*
□ *Personal Motion*

39. You packed.

40. You wouldn't let something go.

41. You enjoyed the morning.

42. You danced well.

43. You amused people because you wanted to.

44. You refused to do what was wanted of you and did what you wanted.

45. You were glad you were you.

46. You were complimented on posture.

Can you recall a time when:

47. You shook hands with somebody you were glad to see.

48. You grabbed something you desired.

49. You combed your hair.

50. You picked up this book.

51. You sat down a little while ago.

□ *Sight*
□ *Smell*
□ *Touch*
□ *Color*
□ *Tone*
□ *External Motion*
□ *Emotion*
□ *Loudness*
□ *Body Position*
□ *Sound*
□ *Weight*
□ *Personal Motion*

MOTION EXTERNAL

The observation of *external motion* is accomplished by many sense channels. The ability to perceive motion in present time and the ability to recall things which have moved and perceive that they are moving are two different things. Inability to perceive well various motions occurring in one's environment is dangerous. But it is caused by the misapprehension that the movements one perceives are dangerous when they most ordinarily are not. For every dangerous motion in one's environment, there are countless thousands of safe and friendly motions. Because motion has been dangerous in the past is no reason to conceive all motion as dangerous. Possibly one of the most aberrative actions, above the level of unconsciousness, is striking a person suddenly when he does not expect it. Slapping children, particularly when they are not alert to the fact that they are about to be slapped, tends to give an individual a distrust of all motion. And even when they become of an age when a slap would be the last thing they would expect, they still continue to distrust motion. In recalling motions you have seen externally, make an effort to see the actual movements which were around you.

□ Sight
□ Smell
□ Touch
□ Color
□ Tone
□ External
   Motion
□ Emotion
□ Loudness
□ Body
   Position
□ Sound
□ Weight
□ Personal
   Motion

Can you recall a time when:

1. Something pleasant moved very fast.

2. You saw somebody you didn't like running away from you.

3. You enjoyed seeing the rain come down.

4. You enjoyed seeing children play.

Can you recall a time when:

5. Trees rustled in a summer wind.

6. A quiet brook flowed.

7. You played ball.

8. You saw a kite flying.

9. You were exhilarated riding downhill.

10. You saw a bird fly gracefully.

11. You perceived the Moon had moved.

12. You scared an animal away from you.

13. You saw a graceful dancer.

14. You saw an accomplished musician.

15. You saw an excellent actor.

16. You watched a graceful girl.

17. You watched a happy child.

☐ *Sight*
☐ *Smell*
☐ *Touch*
☐ *Color*
☐ *Tone*
☐ *External Motion*
☐ *Emotion*
☐ *Loudness*
☐ *Body Position*
☐ *Sound*
☐ *Weight*
☐ *Personal Motion*

Can you recall a time when:

18. You started an object.

19. You stopped an object.

20. You broke something you didn't like.

21. You watched a graceful man.

□ *Sight*
□ *Smell*
□ *Touch*
□ *Color*
□ *Tone*
□ *External Motion*
□ *Emotion*
□ *Loudness*
□ *Body Position*
□ *Sound*
□ *Weight*
□ *Personal Motion*

22. You enjoyed watching a ferocious animal.

23. You were glad to see something fall.

24. You watched something going around and around.

25. You enjoyed bouncing something.

26. You were happy to see something shoot up in the air.

27. You watched a fast horse.

28. You heard something swift.

29. You saw a "shooting star."

Can you recall a time when:

30. You saw grass moving in the wind.

31. You watched the second hand of a clock.

32. You saw somebody you didn't like walk away from you.

33. You saw somebody you liked walk toward you.

□ *Sight*
□ *Smell*
□ *Touch*
□ *Color*
□ *Tone*
□ *External Motion*
□ *Emotion*
□ *Loudness*
□ *Body Position*
□ *Sound*
□ *Weight*
□ *Personal Motion*

34. Somebody ran up and greeted you.

35. You saw an animal chasing an animal.

36. You moved an object.

37. You lifted an object.

38. You threw an object down.

39. You watched a friendly fire.

40. You saw a light come on.

41. You saw something go into something.

Can you recall a time when:

□ *Sight*
□ *Smell*
□ *Touch*
□ *Color*
□ *Tone*
□ *External Motion*
□ *Emotion*
□ *Loudness*
□ *Body Position*
□ *Sound*
□ *Weight*
□ *Personal Motion*

42. You emptied something.

43. You pulled something out.

44. You heard a friendly movement.

45. You destroyed something you didn't want.

46. You turned the page of this book.

BODY POSITION

One is aware of the position of one's body by special perceptions. These include joint position. With the following questions, give particular attention in the incident you recall to the *position of your body* at the time the incident occurred.

Can you recall a time when:

1. You enjoyed just sitting.

2. You fought your way out of a place you didn't want to be.

3. You stood and enjoyed a view.

4. You put your toe in your mouth.

5. You tried to stand on your head.

6. You tried to see if you could be a contortionist.

7. You drank something pleasant.

8. You ate an excellent meal.

9. You drove a good car.

10. You were doing something you liked.

□ *Sight*
□ *Smell*
□ *Touch*
□ *Color*
□ *Tone*
□ *External Motion*
□ *Emotion*
□ *Loudness*
□ *Body Position*
□ *Sound*
□ *Weight*
□ *Personal Motion*

Can you recall a time when:

11. You enjoyed handling something.

12. You were competent in a sport.

13. You were admired.

□ *Sight*
□ *Smell*
□ *Touch*   **14. You were happy.**
□ *Color*
□ *Tone*
□ *External* **15. You enjoyed a chance to sit down.**
  Motion
□ *Emotion*
□ *Loudness* **16. You enthusiastically stood up to go**
□ *Body*   **someplace.**
  Position
□ *Sound*
□ *Weight*   **17. You got rid of something.**
□ *Personal*
  Motion

18. You watched a child being trained.

19. You wanted to stay and did.

20. You wanted to leave and did.

YOU AND THE PHYSICAL UNIVERSE

O ne can consider that the missions of the energy of life, or at least one of them, is the creation, conservation, maintenance, acquisition, destruction, change, occupation, grouping and dispersal of matter, energy, space and time, which are the component factors of the material universe.

So long as an individual maintains his own belief in his ability to handle the physical universe and organisms about him—and to control them if necessary or to work in harmony with them, and to make himself competent over and among the physical universe of his environment—he remains healthy, stable and balanced and cheerful. It is only after he discovers his inabilities in handling organisms, matter, energy, space and time, and when these things have been sharply painful to him, that he begins to decline physically, become less competent mentally and to fail in life. These questions are aimed toward the rehabilitation of his ability to handle organisms and the physical universe.

It was a pre-Dianetic error that an individual was healthy so long as he was adjusted to his environment. Nothing could be less workable than this "adaptive" postulate. And had anyone cared to compare it with actuality, he would have discovered that the success of Man depends upon his ability to master and change his environment. Man succeeds because he adjusts his environment to *him*, not by adjusting himself to the environment.

The "adjusted" postulate is, indeed, a viciously dangerous one, since it seeks to indoctrinate the individual into the belief that he must be a slave to his environment. The philosophy is dangerous because the people so indoctrinated can be enslaved in that last of all graveyards, a welfare state.

However, this postulate is very handy in case one wishes to subjugate or nullify human beings for his own ends. The effort in the direction of adjusting men to their environment, by giving them "social training," by punishing them if they are bad and by otherwise attempting to subdue and break them, has filled the society's prisons and insane asylums to the bursting point. Had anyone cared to look at the real universe, he would have found this to be true: *No living organism can be broken by force into an adjusted state and still remain able and amiable.* Any horse trainer, for instance, knows that the horse must not be pushed or broken into submission if one wishes to retain his abilities. But as they used to say in the army, mules were far more expensive than men, and perhaps it was not in the interest of pre-Dianetic thought to preserve men in a happy state. However, one should not be too harsh on these previous schools of thought since they had no knowledge of the natural laws of thought. And in the absence of these, criminals can only be punished and not cured and the insane can only be driven down into the last dregs of tractability. The nearer to death, according to those schools of thought, the better, as witness electric shock "therapy" and brain surgery—those efforts on the part of the mental medical men to as closely approximate euthanasia as possible without crossing the border into the legal fact of death. These past schools have now been taken under the wing of Dianetics, which embraces all fields of thought, and are being re-educated. It is found that they quickly desert the punishment-drive "therapies" as soon as they completely understand that they are not necessary, now that the natural laws of thought and behavior are known.

One cannot, however, wholly repress a shudder at the fate of the hundreds of thousands of human guinea pigs whose lives and persons were ruined by the euthanistic methods employed in the dark ages of unreason.

Your health depends almost entirely upon your confidence in your ability to handle the physical universe about you and to change and adjust your environment so that you can survive in it. It is actually an illusion that you cannot ably handle your environment—an illusion implanted by aberrated people, in the past, during moments when you were unconscious and could not defend yourself. Or, when you were small and were directed and misdirected and given pain and sorrow and upset and had no way to effect your right to handle yourself in your environment.

On Lake Tanganyika, the natives have a very interesting way of catching fish. There, on the equator, the Sun shines straight down through the clear water. The natives take blocks of wood and string them along a long rope. They stretch this rope between two canoes and, with these abreast, begin to paddle toward the shoal water. By the time they have reached the shoals, schools of fish are piled and crowded into the rocks and onto the beach. The blocks of wood on the rope made shadows which went all the way down to the bottom of the lake. And the fish, seeing the approach of these shadows and the apparent solid bars which they formed in the water, swam fearfully away from them and so were caught.

A man can be driven and harassed and worked upon by aberrated people about him until he, too, conceives shadows to be reality. Should he simply reach out toward them, he would discover how thin and penetrable they are. His usual course, however, is to retreat from them and at last find himself in the shadows of bad health, broken dreams and an utter disownment of himself and the physical universe.

A considerable mechanical background of the action and peculiarities of the energy of thought makes it possible for these lists to bring about the improved state of being that they do, when properly used. But over and above these mechanical aspects, the simple recognition that there have been times in one's life when he did control the physical universe as needful, when he was in harmony with organisms about him, validates the reality of his ability.

Caught up by the illusion of words, stressed into obedience when he was a child by physical means, Man is subject to his greatest shadow and illusion—*language*. The words, forcefully spoken, "Come here!" have no actual physical ability to draw the individual to the speaker. Yet he may approach, although he may be afraid to do so. He is impelled in his approach because he has been made to "come here" by physical force so many times in the early period of his life, while the words "come here" were being spoken, that he is trained much like a dog to obey a signal. The physical force which made him approach is lost to view and in its place stands the shadow "come here." Thus, to that degree, he loses his self-determinism on the subject of "come here."

As life goes on, he makes the great error of supposing that any and all words have force and importance. With words, those about him plant their shadow cages. They restrict him from doing this, they compel him to do that. And, almost hour-by-hour and day-by-day, he is directed by streams of words which in the ordinary society are not meant to help him, but only to restrain him because of the fear of others. This Niagara of language is effective only because it substitutes for periods when he was physically impelled against his wishes to accept things he did not want, to care for things for which he actually had no use or liking, to go where he did not wish to go and to do what he did not want to do.

Language is quite acceptable when understood as a *symbol* for the act and thing. But the word "ashtray" is no substitute for an ashtray. If you do not believe this, try to put your ashes on the airwaves which have just carried the word "ashtray." Called a "saucer" or an "elephant," the object intended for ashes serves just as well.

By the trick of language, then, and a magical wholly unsubstantial trick it is, men seek to order the lives of men for their own advantage. And men caged about by the shadows observe and believe to their own detriment.

All languages derive from observation of matter, energy, space and time and other organisms in the environment. There is no word which is not derived and which does not have the connotation of the physical universe and other organisms.

Thus when you answer these questions—by recalling incidents which they evoke—be very sure that you do not evoke language incidents, but action incidents.

You do *not* want the time when you were *told* to do something—you want the time when you performed the *action*. You do not have to connect the language to the action in any way. But you will find as you answer questions on any of these lists that the value of language begins to depreciate considerably and that language, strangely enough, will become much more useful to you.

Can you recall a time when:

1. You moved an object.

2. An object moved you.

3. You threw an organism up into the air.

4. You walked downstairs.

□ *Sight*
□ *Smell*
□ *Touch*
□ *Color*
□ *Tone*
□ *External Motion*
□ *Emotion*
□ *Loudness*
□ *Body Position*
□ *Sound*
□ *Weight*
□ *Personal Motion*

5. You acquired something you wanted.

6. You created something good.

7. You felt big in a certain space.

8. You were proud to move something heavy.

9. You handled energy well.

10. You built a fire.

11. You lost something you didn't want.

12. You forced something on somebody.

13. You promoted survival.

Can you recall a time when:

14. You pleasantly expended time.

15. You closed in space.

16. You were master of your own time.

17. You opened up a space.

18. You handled a machine well.

19. You stopped a machine.

20. You raised an object.

21. You lowered yourself.

22. You destroyed something you didn't want.

23. You changed something for the better.

24. An organism you did not like moved away from you.

25. You obtained something you wanted.

26. You maintained a person.

☐ *Sight*
☐ *Smell*
☐ *Touch*
☐ *Color*
☐ *Tone*
☐ *External Motion*
☐ *Emotion*
☐ *Loudness*
☐ *Body Position*
☐ *Sound*
☐ *Weight*
☐ *Personal Motion*

Can you recall a time when:

27. You brought somebody you liked close to you.

28. You left a space you didn't like.

29. You conquered energy.

30. You destroyed a bad organism.

□ *Sight*
□ *Smell*
□ *Touch*

31. You handled fluid well.

□ *Color*
□ *Tone*
□ *External Motion*

32. You brought a number of pleasant objects together.

□ *Emotion*
□ *Loudness*
□ *Body Position*

33. You placed a number of objects into space.

□ *Sound*
□ *Weight*
□ *Personal Motion*

34. You threw unwanted objects away.

35. You dispersed many objects.

36. You tore an unwanted object to pieces.

37. You filled a space.

38. You regulated another's time.

Can you recall a time when:

39. You held an object close that you wanted.

40. You improved an object.

41. You emptied a space you wanted.

42. You went a distance.

43. You let time go.

44. You did what you wanted to do yourself.

45. You won out over an organism.

46. You got out from under domination.

47. You realized you were living your own life.

48. You knew you didn't have to do it.

49. You escaped from a dangerous space.

50. You entered upon a pleasant time.

☐ *Sight*
☐ *Smell*
☐ *Touch*
☐ *Color*
☐ *Tone*
☐ *External Motion*
☐ *Emotion*
☐ *Loudness*
☐ *Body Position*
☐ *Sound*
☐ *Weight*
☐ *Personal Motion*

ASSISTS TO REMEMBERING

"Remember" is derived, of course, directly from action in the physical universe. How would a deaf-mute teach a child to remember? It would be necessary for him to keep forcing objects or actions on the child when the child left them alone or omitted them. Although parents are not deaf-mutes, children do not understand languages at very early ages and, as a consequence, learn to "remember" by having their attention first called toward actions and objects, spaces and time. It violates the self-determinism of the individual, and therefore his ability to handle himself, to have things forced upon him without his agreement. This could be said to account, in part, for some of the "poor memories" about which people brag or complain.

Because one learns language at the level of the physical universe and action within it, he could be said to do with his thoughts what he has been compelled to do with the matter, energy, space and time in his environment. Thus, if these have been forced upon him and he did not want them, after a while he will begin to reject the thoughts concerning these objects.

But if these objects, spaces and times and actions are forced upon him consistently enough, he will at length go into an apathy about them. He will not want them very much, but he thinks he has to accept them. Later on, in school, his whole livelihood seems to depend on whether or not he can remember the "knowledge" which is forced upon him.

The physical universe level of remembering, then, is retaining matter, energy, space and time. To improve the memory, it is only necessary to rehabilitate the individual's choice of acceptance of the material universe.

In answering these questions, particular attention should be paid to the happier incidents. Inevitably, many unhappy incidents will flick through. But where selection is possible, happy or analytical incidents should be stressed. This list does not pertain to asking you to remember times when you remembered. It pertains to acquiring things which you wanted to acquire.

Can you remember a time when:

1. You acquired something you wanted.

2. You threw away something you didn't want.

3. You abandoned something you knew you were supposed to have.

4. You did something else with the time which was otherwise appointed for you.

5. You went into a space you were not supposed to occupy.

6. You left the place you were supposed to be.

7. You were happy to have acquired something you couldn't afford.

8. You happily defied directions you had been given.

9. You were sent to one place and chose to go to another.

10. You chose your own clothing.

11. You wore something in spite of what people would think.

□ *Sight*
□ *Smell*
□ *Touch*
□ *Color*
□ *Tone*
□ *External Motion*
□ *Emotion*
□ *Loudness*
□ *Body Position*
□ *Sound*
□ *Weight*
□ *Personal Motion*

Can you remember a time when:

12. You got rid of something which bored you.

13. You were glad to have choice over one of two objects.

14. You didn't drink any more than you wanted to.

□ *Sight*
□ *Smell*
□ *Touch*
□ *Color*
□ *Tone*
□ *External Motion*
□ *Emotion*
□ *Loudness*
□ *Body Position*
□ *Sound*
□ *Weight*
□ *Personal Motion*

15. You successfully refused to eat.

16. You did what you pleased with yourself.

17. You did what you pleased with a smaller person.

18. You were right not to have accepted something.

19. You gave away a present you had received.

20. You destroyed an object somebody forced upon you.

21. You had something you wanted and maintained it well.

22. You maliciously scuffed your shoes.

Can you remember a time when:

23. You didn't read the book you had been given.

24. You refused to be owned.

25. You changed somebody's orders.

26. You slept where you pleased.

27. You refused to bathe.

28. You spoiled some clothing and were cheerful about it.

29. You got what you wanted.

30. You got back something you had lost.

31. You got the person you wanted.

32. You refused a partner.

33. You threw the blankets off the bed.

34. You had your own way.

35. You found you had been right in refusing it.

☐ *Sight*
☐ *Smell*
☐ *Touch*
☐ *Color*
☐ *Tone*
☐ *External Motion*
☐ *Emotion*
☐ *Loudness*
☐ *Body Position*
☐ *Sound*
☐ *Weight*
☐ *Personal Motion*

FORGETTER SECTION

It is generally conceded that the opposite of *to remember* is *to forget*. People can easily become confused between these two things, so that they forget what they think they should remember and remember what they think they should forget. The basic and underlying confusion between *forget* and *remember* has to do, evidently, with what has been done to the individual on a physical level and what has been forced on him or taken away from him in terms of matter, energy, space and time.

The word "forget" rests, for its definition, on the action of leaving something alone. How would a deaf-mute teach a child to forget something? He would, of course, have to hide it or consistently take it away from a child until the child went into apathy about it and would have nothing further to do with it. If he did this enough, so that the child would abandon the object, a child could be said to have forgotten the object, since the child, or any person, will do with his thoughts what he has done with the matter, energy, space, time and organisms around him—thoughts being an approximation in symbological form of the physical universe. If a child has been forcefully made to leave alone or abandon objects, energy, spaces and times, later on when he hears the word "forget," this means he must abandon a certain thought. And if he is in apathy concerning the forced loss of objects or having them taken away from him in childhood, he will proceed to forget them very thoroughly.

It could be said that an individual will occlude as many thoughts as he has had to leave alone or lose objects in life. Pain itself is a loss, being uniformly accompanied by the loss of cells of the body. Thus the loss of objects, or organisms, by the individual can be misconstrued as being painful. Memories then can be called "painful" which actually contain no physical pain. But the individual must have had physical pain in order to understand that the loss means pain.

Punishment often accompanies, in child training, the times when the child is supposed to leave something alone. Thus, having to leave something alone is equivalent to being painful. Thus, to remember something one is supposed to forget could be erroneously judged to be painful and, indeed, it is not.

There is a whole philosophy in existence that the best thing to do with unpleasant thoughts is to forget them. This is based securely upon an apathy occasioned by early training. A child, when asking for an object, will usually at first be cheerful. And when he does not procure it, will become angry. If he still does not procure it, he may cry. And, at last, goes into apathy concerning it and says that he does not want it. This is one of the derivations of the Dianetic Tone Scale and can be observed by anyone.

These questions, then, are an effort to overcome the times when one has had to leave things alone, when one has had to lose things and when the loss has been enforced. Thus, when answering these questions, it would be very well to try to find several incidents for each, particularly a very early incident.

Can you recall an incident when:

1. You put something aside because you thought it was dangerous but it wasn't.

2. You acquired something you were not supposed to have and kept it.

3. You cheerfully got into everything you were supposed to leave alone.

4. You went back to something you had been pulled away from.

5. You found the caution to leave something alone groundless.

6. You cheerfully destroyed an expensive object.

7. You threw away something you wanted.

8. You played with somebody you were supposed to leave alone.

9. You were right in disobeying.

10. You read a forbidden book.

11. You enjoyed having things.

☐ *Sight*
☐ *Smell*
☐ *Touch*
☐ *Color*
☐ *Tone*
☐ *External Motion*
☐ *Emotion*
☐ *Loudness*
☐ *Body Position*
☐ *Sound*
☐ *Weight*
☐ *Personal Motion*

Can you recall an incident when:

12. You acquired a dangerous object and enjoyed it.

13. You stole some food and were cheerful about it.

14. You ate exactly what you pleased.

15. You fixed some electrical wiring successfully.

16. You played with fire.

17. You successfully drove dangerously.

18. You touched something in spite of all warnings.

19. You got away with it.

20. She walked out on you.

21. You and some friends collected objects.

22. You touched a forbidden thing happily.

23. You got it anyway.

□ *Sight*
□ *Smell*
□ *Touch*
□ *Color*
□ *Tone*
□ *External Motion*
□ *Emotion*
□ *Loudness*
□ *Body Position*
□ *Sound*
□ *Weight*
□ *Personal Motion*

Can you recall an incident when:

24. You went where you weren't supposed to and enjoyed it.

25. You owned something that was once forbidden.

26. He walked out on you.

27. You threw away something you had had to accept.

28. You found something which had been hidden from you.

29. You acquired a habit you weren't supposed to have and enjoyed it.

30. You were right and they were wrong.

31. You enjoyed yourself in a forbidden space.

32. You weren't supposed to do it and you did.

33. People were glad they had been wrong about you.

□ *Sight*
□ *Smell*
□ *Touch*
□ *Color*
□ *Tone*
□ *External Motion*
□ *Emotion*
□ *Loudness*
□ *Body Position*
□ *Sound*
□ *Weight*
□ *Personal Motion*

Can you recall an incident when:

34. You recovered something somebody had thrown away.

35. You bullied somebody into giving you something you wanted.

36. You kept on with this processing despite what was said.

□ *Sight*
□ *Smell*
□ *Touch*
□ *Color*
□ *Tone*
□ *External Motion*
□ *Emotion*
□ *Loudness*
□ *Body Position*
□ *Sound*
□ *Weight*
□ *Personal Motion*

37. You persisted in doing something until they agreed you had a right to.

38. You suddenly realized you could do anything you wanted with an object.

39. You did something dangerous and got away with it.

40. Your group finally got something they had been denied.

41. You found you didn't have to sit there anymore.

42. You realized you didn't have to go to school ever again.

43. You realized it was recess.

Can you recall an incident when:

44. You played hooky.

45. You made something look like something else.

46. You found where an adult had made a mistake.

47. You discovered it wasn't what they said it was.

48. You found yourself master of all of your possessions.

49. You discovered you didn't necessarily have to go to sleep at night.

50. Although you felt you had to eat it, you left it alone.

51. You ate something that wasn't good for you and enjoyed it.

52. You let yourself get mad and were glad of it.

53. You suddenly decided you couldn't be that bad.

☐ *Sight*
☐ *Smell*
☐ *Touch*
☐ *Color*
☐ *Tone*
☐ *External Motion*
☐ *Emotion*
☐ *Loudness*
☐ *Body Position*
☐ *Sound*
☐ *Weight*
☐ *Personal Motion*

Can you recall an incident when:

54. You opened a forbidden door.

55. You made it go very fast when it should have gone slow.

56. You stole some time.

57. You found some love you didn't know was there.

□ *Sight*

□ *Smell*

□ *Touch*

□ *Color*

58. You abandoned somebody and were glad of it.

□ *Tone*

□ *External Motion*

□ *Emotion*

59. You refused to leave that time alone.

□ *Loudness*

□ *Body Position*

□ *Sound*

60. You sneaked off and built a fire.

□ *Weight*

□ *Personal Motion*

61. You didn't realize it could be that good.

62. You found out it wasn't bad to play.

63. You couldn't see what was wrong with pleasure.

64. You left off doing something you were supposed to do, to do something you enjoyed.

Can you recall an incident when:

65. You acquired a space you once wouldn't have had.

66. You indulged yourself thoroughly.

67. They couldn't keep you back from it.

68. You successfully refused to come to the table.

69. You got burned anyway and didn't care.

70. You got rid of an object and acquired liberty.

□ *Sight*
□ *Smell*
□ *Touch*
□ *Color*
□ *Tone*
□ *External Motion*
□ *Emotion*
□ *Loudness*
□ *Body Position*
□ *Sound*
□ *Weight*
□ *Personal Motion*

SURVIVAL
FACTORS

In that the basic drive of life is SURVIVAL! and in that good survival must contain an abundance, the survival characteristics of people, organisms, matter, energy, space and time, from the viewpoint of an individual, are very important. The incentive toward survival is the acquisition of pleasure. The thrust away from death is the threat of pain. High ideals and ethics enhance the potentialities of the individual and the group in surviving. The ultimate in survival is immortality.

The factors which make up life can become contradictory in that one item can, in itself, assist survival and inhibit survival. A knife, for instance, is pro-survival in the hand, but contra-survival when pointed at the breast by somebody else. As a person advances in life, he becomes confused as to the survival value of certain persons, various objects, energy, space and time. The individual desires survival for himself, for his family, for his children, for his group, for life in general and the physical universe. Confusing one thing with another and beholding an item which was once survival become non-survival, beholding non-survival entities taking on survival qualities, the ability of the individual to evaluate his environment in terms of whether it assists or inhibits survival deteriorates.

An individual, a family, a group best survives, of course, when pro-survival entities are in proximity and available and when contra-survival entities are absent. The struggle of life could be said to be the procurement of pro-survival factors and the annihilation, destruction, banishment of contra-survival factors.

Emotion is directly regulated by pro-survival and contra-survival factors in life. When an individual procures and has in his proximity a strong survival entity, such as another person or animal or object, he is *happy*. As this pro-survival entity departs from him, his emotional reaction deteriorates in direct ratio to his belief in his ability to recover it. As it threatens to depart, he becomes *antagonistic* and fights to keep it near him. If its departure seems certain, he will become *angry* and, lest it become pro-survival for another life form and he is assured he has lost it, he will even destroy it. When he realizes what his own state may be—or the state of his family, children or group—with his pro-survival entity departed, he experiences *fear* that its loss will be permanent. When he recognizes what he believes to be a nearly irretrievable absence of this pro-survival entity, he experiences *grief*. When it is considered to be lost permanently, he experiences *apathy* and, in apathy, he may even go to the point of saying he did not want it. Actually, from antagonism on down the Tone Scale of emotion all the way to grief, he is still fighting to get it back. And only in apathy, abandons it and negates against it.

In the case of a person, animal, object, energy, space or time which threatens the survival of an individual, his family, his children or his group, the best survival can be accomplished when such an entity has been banished or destroyed or is as distant as possible from the individual, his family, his children or his group. In the case of the mad dog, the greatest danger exists when he is nearest and the greatest safety exists when he is most distant or absent. With contra-survival objects, then, we have the Tone Scale in reverse. When the contra-survival object is present and cannot be put away, the individual experiences *apathy*. When the individual believes himself to be threatened or when he feels his family, his children or his group are threatened by a contra-survival object to a point where he cannot easily repel it, *grief* is experienced (for grief contains some hope of victory through enlisting the sympathy of one's allies). When a contra-survival entity is threatening to approach, *fear* is experienced, providing one feels that a direct attack is not possible. If the contra-survival object is near, but the individual, his family, his children or his group feel that it can be conquered even though it is already too close, *anger* results. If a contra-survival entity might possibly approach, *antagonism* is demonstrated. Above this level, contra-survival objects may be more and more distant or easily handled up to the point where the individual can even be cheerful about them, at which time they are either absent or can be handled with ease.

Individuals get into a fixed emotional state about their environment when contra-survival objects remain too statically in their environment or when pro-survival objects are too difficult to obtain and cannot be procured or brought near or seem inclined to leave. Mixed with these emotional states is the confusion occasioned by a dulled ability to differentiate between the pro- and contra-survival of an entity.

A parent is contra-survival in that he punishes, is much too big and cannot be contributed to, which lessens the survival potentialities of a child. On the other hand, the same parent furnishing food, clothing and shelter and also, but not least, being an entity which loves and can be loved, is a pro-survival entity. The parent entirely absent, then, is not a satisfactory survival state. The parent present is not a satisfactory survival state.

Hence an indecision results and the individual demonstrates anxiety toward the parent. But this anxiety exists because of many hidden situations extending back to the beginning of an individual's life.

The following questions are designed so as to permit the individual to reevaluate the pro-survival and contra-survival nature of persons, animals, objects, energies, space and time in general.

LIST 7
SURVIVAL FACTORS

Can you recall a time when:

1. **A person you disliked was about.**

2. **An individual you liked stood above you.**

3. **You finally accepted a person you liked.**

4. **You enjoyed accompanying a person you liked.**

5. **You were against a person you liked.**

6. **You acquired an individual you liked.**

7. **You and a person you liked engaged in a pleasant action.**

8. **Your action resulted in getting rid of somebody you didn't like.**

9. **You enjoyed seeing somebody you admired.**

10. **You advanced toward a person you liked.**

11. **You acquired an object which you adored.**

☐ *Sight*
☐ *Smell*
☐ *Touch*
☐ *Color*
☐ *Tone*
☐ *External Motion*
☐ *Emotion*
☐ *Loudness*
☐ *Body Position*
☐ *Sound*
☐ *Weight*
☐ *Personal Motion*

Can you recall a time when:

12. You knew somebody felt affection for you.

13. You got away from a person of whom you were afraid.

14. You walked after a person you liked.

□ *Sight*
□ *Smell*
□ *Touch*
□ *Color*
□ *Tone*
□ *External Motion*
□ *Emotion*
□ *Loudness*
□ *Body Position*
□ *Sound*
□ *Weight*
□ *Personal Motion*

15. A person you liked aided you.

16. You and people you liked were all together.

17. You almost met somebody you disliked.

18. You were glad to be alone.

19. Somebody aided your ambition.

20. You were among people you liked.

21. You found somebody amiable.

22. A person amused you.

23. You finally didn't have to be anxious.

Can you recall a time when:

24. A person you liked appeared suddenly.

25. You had a good appetite.

26. You approached somebody you honored.

27. Somebody approved of you.

28. A person you liked arose.

29. You were arrested by somebody's beauty.

30. You enjoyed an arrival.

31. You found out you didn't have to be ashamed.

32. Somebody you liked was asleep.

33. You assailed an enemy successfully.

34. A person you honored assisted you.

35. You enjoyed an associate.

36. You felt assured by a person you liked.

□ *Sight*
□ *Smell*
□ *Touch*
□ *Color*
□ *Tone*
□ *External Motion*
□ *Emotion*
□ *Loudness*
□ *Body Position*
□ *Sound*
□ *Weight*
□ *Personal Motion*

Can you recall a time when:

37. You were astonished to find out somebody respected you after all.

38. You attacked somebody you didn't like.

39. You were attached to a friend.

□ *Sight*
□ *Smell*
□ *Touch*
□ *Color*
□ *Tone*
□ *External Motion*
□ *Emotion*
□ *Loudness*
□ *Body Position*
□ *Sound*
□ *Weight*
□ *Personal Motion*

40. Somebody you liked gave you attention.

41. You were attractive to somebody.

42. You were awakened by somebody of whom you were fond.

43. You were glad to find somebody was bad.

44. You played ball.

45. You played a battle with children.

46. Somebody considered you beautiful.

47. You discovered you had become fond of someone.

48. Somebody you disliked begged you.

Can you recall a time when:

49. You began a friendship.

50. You discovered you didn't have to behave.

51. A person you disliked was behind you.

52. You were below somebody you liked.

53. Somebody of whom you were fond bested you.

54. You were beside your favorite friend.

55. You discovered you were liked better than you thought.

56. You were between two friends.

57. You bit somebody you disliked.

58. You decided to be blind to a fault.

59. You liked somebody who was of another race.

60. Somebody asked you to blow hard.

□ *Sight*
□ *Smell*
□ *Touch*
□ *Color*
□ *Tone*
□ *External Motion*
□ *Emotion*
□ *Loudness*
□ *Body Position*
□ *Sound*
□ *Weight*
□ *Personal Motion*

Can you recall a time when:

61. Somebody's question made you blush pleasantly.

62. Somebody made you feel bold.

63. You were glad somebody had been born.

□ *Sight*
□ *Smell*
□ *Touch*
□ *Color*
□ *Tone*
□ *External Motion*
□ *Emotion*
□ *Loudness*
□ *Body Position*
□ *Sound*
□ *Weight*
□ *Personal Motion*

64. Nobody could bother you.

65. You had reached the bottom and started up.

66. You bowed to a friend.

67. You were in a box with a pleasant person.

68. You broke bread with somebody you liked.

69. You breakfasted with somebody you liked.

70. You liked somebody so much you could hardly breathe.

71. You brought somebody a present.

Can you recall a time when:

72. You brushed against somebody you liked.

73. Somebody helped you build something.

74. Somebody kissed a burn.

75. You were so happy you felt you would burst.

76. You buried something you didn't want.

77. You were too busy to see an enemy.

78. You stood by somebody.

79. You saw something you disliked in a cage.

80. You answered a call from a friend.

81. You broke a cane.

82. You captured an enemy.

83. You no longer had to be careful.

☐ *Sight*
☐ *Smell*
☐ *Touch*
☐ *Color*
☐ *Tone*
☐ *External Motion*
☐ *Emotion*
☐ *Loudness*
☐ *Body Position*
☐ *Sound*
☐ *Weight*
☐ *Personal Motion*

Can you recall a time when:

84. You found somebody cared.

85. You enjoyed being careless.

86. A cat you didn't like walked away from you.

87. You discovered you weren't the cause.

□ *Sight*
□ *Smell*
□ *Touch*
□ *Color*
□ *Tone*
□ *External Motion*
□ *Emotion*
□ *Loudness*
□ *Body Position*
□ *Sound*
□ *Weight*
□ *Personal Motion*

88. They couldn't catch you and you realized it.

89. You were certain of a friend.

90. You discovered you had charm.

91. You enjoyed a child.

92. You found a church pleasant.

93. You discovered there were friends in the city.

94. You and others left the classroom.

95. Somebody believed you clever.

96. You found an enemy was clumsy.

Can you recall a time when:

97. You didn't have to clothe yourself as directed.

98. You threw away a collar.

99. You didn't have to comb your hair.

100. You were comfortable with a person.

101. You saw an enemy coming and didn't meet him.

102. You could come as you pleased.

103. An enemy had to obey your command.

104. You found you were in command.

105. You heard an enemy was committed.

106. You were in good company.

107. You took compassion on an enemy.

108. You were discovered to be a good companion.

□ *Sight*
□ *Smell*
□ *Touch*
□ *Color*
□ *Tone*
□ *External Motion*
□ *Emotion*
□ *Loudness*
□ *Body Position*
□ *Sound*
□ *Weight*
□ *Personal Motion*

Can you recall a time when:

109. You felt complete.

110. You concealed yourself from an enemy.

111. You condemned an enemy.

112. People had confidence in you.

☐ *Sight*
☐ *Smell*
☐ *Touch*
☐ *Color*
☐ *Tone*
☐ *External Motion*
☐ *Emotion*
☐ *Loudness*
☐ *Body Position*
☐ *Sound*
☐ *Weight*
☐ *Personal Motion*

113. You confounded an enemy.

114. You conquered an enemy physically.

115. Somebody consented.

116. You couldn't contain yourself.

117. You saw an enemy contract.

118. You proved very contrary.

119. It was hard to count your friends.

120. People realized you had courage.

121. Your courting was successful.

Can you recall a time when:

122. You put a cover over an enemy.

123. You made an enemy crawl.

124. You created a group.

125. You made somebody get over being cross.

☐ *Sight*
☐ *Smell*
☐ *Touch*
☐ *Color*
☐ *Tone*
☐ *External Motion*
☐ *Emotion*
☐ *Loudness*
☐ *Body Position*
☐ *Sound*
☐ *Weight*
☐ *Personal Motion*

126. You were glad to be in a crowd.

127. You made an enemy cry.

128. You cured a friend.

129. An enemy cut himself.

130. You lost an enemy in the dark.

131. You discovered something you didn't like was dead.

132. You turned a deaf ear to an enemy.

133. You forgave somebody for deceiving you.

Can you recall a time when:

134. You threw somebody you didn't like into dejection.

135. You delayed a catastrophe.

136. Somebody was delighted with you.

137. You could not deny a favor.

□ *Sight*
□ *Smell*
□ *Touch*
□ *Color*
□ *Tone*
□ *External Motion*
□ *Emotion*
□ *Loudness*
□ *Body Position*
□ *Sound*
□ *Weight*
□ *Personal Motion*

138. You could not deny what you wanted.

139. You overlooked a defect in a friend.

140. You were depended upon.

141. An enemy got what he deserved.

142. Your desire was answered.

143. You departed from an enemy.

144. An enemy departed from you.

145. You drove an enemy into despair.

146. You and another successfully reached a destination.

Can you recall a time when:

147. Your group destroyed an enemy.

148. Your determination won.

149. You could tell the difference.

150. You diminished an enemy.

151. You dispersed a group you didn't like.

152. You found you were right to distrust somebody.

153. You dived in.

154. There was plenty to divide.

155. You had no doubt of someone.

156. You drove somebody.

157. You and a friendly person ate.

158. Your effort was rewarded.

159. You were enclosed by friends.

□ Sight
□ Smell
□ Touch
□ Color
□ Tone
□ External Motion
□ Emotion
□ Loudness
□ Body Position
□ Sound
□ Weight
□ Personal Motion

Can you recall a time when:

160. You successfully encouraged somebody.

161. You put an end to something you didn't like.

162. You enjoyed watching somebody leave.

□ *Sight*
□ *Smell*
□ *Touch*
□ *Color*
□ *Tone*
□ *External Motion*
□ *Emotion*
□ *Loudness*
□ *Body Position*
□ *Sound*
□ *Weight*
□ *Personal Motion*

163. You knew you'd had enough and took action.

164. Somebody was entranced with you.

165. You were equal to anyone.

166. You escaped from an enemy.

167. You got even with somebody you didn't like.

168. You passed an examination in spite of somebody.

169. You were excited by an arrival.

170. Somebody you didn't like escaped from you.

Can you recall a time when:

171. Somebody you disliked went far away.

172. You discovered a person had been faithful.

173. You discovered you didn't have to be afraid anymore.

174. You fed somebody.

175. You discovered your enemies were few.

176. You found somebody you had been looking for.

177. You decided to stick to the finish.

178. Your first enemy went away from you.

179. You watched a detested person flee.

180. You forbade somebody to come near you and were obeyed.

181. You used force on somebody successfully.

182. You realized you were free.

☐ *Sight*
☐ *Smell*
☐ *Touch*
☐ *Color*
☐ *Tone*
☐ *External Motion*
☐ *Emotion*
☐ *Loudness*
☐ *Body Position*
☐ *Sound*
☐ *Weight*
☐ *Personal Motion*

Can you recall a time when:

183. You knew you had a friend.

184. You frightened somebody you didn't like.

185. You gathered friends together.

186. You could go outside the gate.

☐ *Sight*

☐ *Smell*

☐ *Touch*   **187. People found you generous.**

☐ *Color*

☐ *Tone*

☐ *External*   **188. You no longer had to be on your**
Motion   **guard.**

☐ *Emotion*

☐ *Loudness*

☐ *Body*   **189. People made you happy.**
Position

☐ *Sound*

☐ *Weight*   **190. You harmed a person you didn't like.**

☐ *Personal*
Motion

191. Somebody you liked hastened to you.

192. You healed a friend.

193. You helped an ally.

194. You had a friend.

195. You hindered an enemy.

Can you recall a time when:

196. Somebody tossed you up high.

197. You put an enemy in the hole.

198. You agreed it was hot.

199. You hunted an enemy.

200. You hurried toward a group.

201. You hurt somebody you needed.

202. You coaxed somebody into being idle.

203. You illuminated a group.

204. You discovered you had imagined a wrong about someone.

205. You and a friend did the impossible.

206. Somebody you had hunted walked in.

207. You found an enemy ignorant.

208. You made somebody you didn't like impatient.

209. You were discovered to be interesting.

☐ *Sight*
☐ *Smell*
☐ *Touch*
☐ *Color*
☐ *Tone*
☐ *External Motion*
☐ *Emotion*
☐ *Loudness*
☐ *Body Position*
☐ *Sound*
☐ *Weight*
☐ *Personal Motion*

Can you recall a time when:

210. Your invention was appreciated.

211. You took a pleasant journey.

212. You made somebody joyful.

213. You jumped.

☐ *Sight*
☐ *Smell*
☐ *Touch*
☐ *Color*
☐ *Tone*
☐ *External Motion*
☐ *Emotion*
☐ *Loudness*
☐ *Body Position*
☐ *Sound*
☐ *Weight*
☐ *Personal Motion*

214. You kept somebody from doing wrong.

215. You saw an enemy kicked out.

216. You overcame a desire to kill.

217. Somebody found you were kind.

218. You were first kissed.

219. You landed on your feet.

220. You were late and it didn't matter.

221. You made people laugh.

222. You and a person you liked were lazy.

Can you recall a time when:

223. You left an enemy.

224. There was one less.

225. You caught an enemy in a lie.

226. You and your group enjoyed life.

227. You were glad it was light.

228. You were happy to listen.

229. You overcame somebody bigger than you.

230. You made somebody glad to be alive.

231. You found love really existed.

232. Your luck was excellent.

233. You fixed a machine for somebody.

234. You received pleasant mail.

235. You knew a good man.

☐ *Sight*
☐ *Smell*
☐ *Touch*
☐ *Color*
☐ *Tone*
☐ *External Motion*
☐ *Emotion*
☐ *Loudness*
☐ *Body Position*
☐ *Sound*
☐ *Weight*
☐ *Personal Motion*

Can you recall a time when:

236. Somebody imitated your manner.

237. You had an enemy under your control.

238. You decided not to marry.

239. You found you were the master.

□ *Sight*
□ *Smell*
□ *Touch*
□ *Color*
□ *Tone*
□ *External Motion*
□ *Emotion*
□ *Loudness*
□ *Body Position*
□ *Sound*
□ *Weight*
□ *Personal Motion*

240. You discovered you weren't mean.

241. You had a happy meeting.

242. You were in the midst of friends.

243. A person you didn't like minded you.

244. A friend interested you with music.

245. People found you mysterious.

246. You discovered nobody disliked you.

247. You could make all the noise you pleased.

248. You didn't have to obey.

249. You obliged somebody.

Can you recall a time when:

250. You discovered you had not been observed, after all.

251. You made it a gala occasion.

252. You offended somebody you didn't like.

253. You sat on somebody.

254. You shut the door on an enemy.

☐ *Sight*
☐ *Smell*
☐ *Touch*
☐ *Color*
☐ *Tone*
☐ *External Motion*
☐ *Emotion*
☐ *Loudness*
☐ *Body Position*
☐ *Sound*
☐ *Weight*
☐ *Personal Motion*

255. You disobeyed an order and found it was all right.

256. You organized a game.

257. You were glad to participate.

258. You were happy in a partner.

259. You took somebody's part.

260. Somebody experienced passion for you.

261. You were patient with a foolish person.

262. You brought peace.

Can you recall a time when:

263. You felt pity for an enemy.

264. You were impolite and it served your purpose.

265. You found you weren't poor.

266. You took position beside a friend.

□ *Sight*
□ *Smell*
□ *Touch*
□ *Color*
□ *Tone*
□ *External Motion*
□ *Emotion*
□ *Loudness*
□ *Body Position*
□ *Sound*
□ *Weight*
□ *Personal Motion*

267. You felt powerful in your friends.

268. You found somebody was precious to you.

269. You did what you preferred to do with a person.

270. You gave somebody you liked a present.

271. You prevented somebody from doing something foolish.

272. Somebody thought you were pretty.

273. You found you didn't want to see somebody go to prison.

Can you recall a time when:

274. You were right in standing by your principles.

275. You were part of a procession.

276. They discovered you could produce.

277. You and a friend made progress.

278. Somebody was true to a promise.

279. Proof wasn't necessary.

280. Somebody was proud of you.

281. You stayed with your purpose.

282. You were discovered to be of good quality.

283. You stopped a quarrel.

284. You found you could act quickly.

285. It was unnecessary to be quiet.

286. You lifted a child.

☐ *Sight*
☐ *Smell*
☐ *Touch*
☐ *Color*
☐ *Tone*
☐ *External Motion*
☐ *Emotion*
☐ *Loudness*
☐ *Body Position*
☐ *Sound*
☐ *Weight*
☐ *Personal Motion*

Can you recall a time when:

287. You discovered enmity was rare.

288. Somebody read to you.

289. There was danger and you were ready.

290. Somebody unexpectedly reappeared.

□ *Sight*
□ *Smell*
□ *Touch*
□ *Color*
□ *Tone*
□ *External Motion*
□ *Emotion*
□ *Loudness*
□ *Body Position*
□ *Sound*
□ *Weight*
□ *Personal Motion*

291. You received somebody you liked.

292. You recognized a friend.

293. Somebody took refuge in you.

294. You discovered your regrets were in vain.

295. People rejoiced with you.

296. A friend rejoined you.

297. A person decided to remain.

298. You were considered remarkable.

299. You repeated something and weren't sorry for it.

Can you recall a time when:

300. People found you had been wrongly represented.

301. Somebody said you resembled somebody.

302. You found you didn't have to respect somebody.

303. You restored a friendship.

304. You retained goodwill.

305. You revealed trickery.

306. A friend rubbed against you.

307. You tried to save somebody you disliked from ruin.

308. You made an unfriendly person run.

309. You cured somebody's sadness.

310. You discovered safety.

311. You knew you were part of a pretty scene.

□ *Sight*
□ *Smell*
□ *Touch*
□ *Color*
□ *Tone*
□ *External Motion*
□ *Emotion*
□ *Loudness*
□ *Body Position*
□ *Sound*
□ *Weight*
□ *Personal Motion*

Can you recall a time when:

312. You were right in claiming somebody was a scoundrel.

313. You made an unfriendly person scream.

314. You were happy to find somebody wasn't what he seemed.

☐ *Sight*
☐ *Smell*
☐ *Touch*
☐ *Color*
☐ *Tone*
☐ *External Motion*
☐ *Emotion*
☐ *Loudness*
☐ *Body Position*
☐ *Sound*
☐ *Weight*
☐ *Personal Motion*

315. You found you didn't think about yourself all the time, after all.

316. You sent somebody away.

317. You found a person wasn't as severe as you had thought.

318. You made somebody shake.

319. You shouted with joy.

320. You enjoyed shutting something up.

321. You had a friend at your side.

322. You enjoyed the sight of a person leaving.

Can you recall a time when:

323. You forced silence.

324. You found your size didn't matter.

325. Somebody found you were skillful.

326. You were glad you had been slow.

327. You succeeded in putting a puzzle together.

328. You were glad something was slippery.

329. You were glad you came too soon.

330. Somebody was sore at you and it didn't do any good.

331. You tied somebody to a stake.

332. You enjoyed startling somebody.

333. You found you didn't have to starve.

334. You didn't want to stay and didn't.

335. Somebody stuck to you.

☐ *Sight*
☐ *Smell*
☐ *Touch*
☐ *Color*
☐ *Tone*
☐ *External Motion*
☐ *Emotion*
☐ *Loudness*
☐ *Body Position*
☐ *Sound*
☐ *Weight*
☐ *Personal Motion*

Can you recall a time when:

336. Somebody was still your friend.

337. Somebody stirred you.

338. You stopped over to talk to somebody.

339. You stopped an unfriendly person.

□ *Sight*
□ *Smell*
□ *Touch*
□ *Color*
□ *Tone*
□ *External Motion*
□ *Emotion*
□ *Loudness*
□ *Body Position*
□ *Sound*
□ *Weight*
□ *Personal Motion*

340. Somebody you liked in a store was good to you.

341. Somebody made you feel less strong.

342. You stripped an unfriendly person.

343. Somebody stroked you.

344. Somebody discovered how strong you were.

345. You won a struggle.

346. You subdued an unkind person.

347. You found you had a subject.

348. You made an unfriendly person submit.

349. You succeeded in spite of people.

Can you recall a time when:

350. You made a person suffer with justice.

351. You gave another person a suit.

352. You felt sure in the presence of somebody.

353. You handled somebody well.

354. You seized an unfriendly person.

355. Your search was rewarded.

356. Somebody tried to send you away and you didn't go.

357. You found you had taken somebody too seriously.

358. You watched an unfriendly person move fast.

359. You found shame wasn't necessary.

360. Somebody discovered they had suspected you wrongly.

☐ *Sight*
☐ *Smell*
☐ *Touch*
☐ *Color*
☐ *Tone*
☐ *External Motion*
☐ *Emotion*
☐ *Loudness*
☐ *Body Position*
☐ *Sound*
☐ *Weight*
☐ *Personal Motion*

Can you recall a time when:

361. You should have told and you did.

362. Your anxiety was for nothing.

363. You apprehended an unfriendly person.

364. You were glad somebody was tall.

□ *Sight*
□ *Smell*
□ *Touch*
□ *Color*
□ *Tone*
□ *External Motion*
□ *Emotion*
□ *Loudness*
□ *Body Position*
□ *Sound*
□ *Weight*
□ *Personal Motion*

365. Your tears were followed by relief.

366. You terrified an unfriendly person.

367. They had to admit you hadn't stolen it after all.

368. Somebody had to respect your rights of ownership.

369. You tried an unfriendly person out.

370. You got together with an unfriendly person and won.

371. You treated many people.

372. You were glad it was true.

Can you recall a time when:

373. You found it was all right to be under someone.

374. You discovered you weren't an unhappy person.

375. You discovered the difference between "no" and "know."

376. You lifted up a child.

377. You enjoyed going upstairs with somebody.

378. You were found to be useful.

379. Something you thought was rare turned out to be usual.

380. You discovered it was all right to be vain.

381. They discovered how valuable you were.

382. You found something wasn't a vice.

383. You recovered your vigor.

□ *Sight*
□ *Smell*
□ *Touch*
□ *Color*
□ *Tone*
□ *External Motion*
□ *Emotion*
□ *Loudness*
□ *Body Position*
□ *Sound*
□ *Weight*
□ *Personal Motion*

Can you recall a time when:

384. You overcame a violent person.

385. You found you had no invisible enemies.

386. You made a dog wag his tail.

387. You really earned the wages you were paid.

☐ *Sight*
☐ *Smell*
☐ *Touch*
☐ *Color*
☐ *Tone*
☐ *External Motion*
☐ *Emotion*
☐ *Loudness*
☐ *Body Position*
☐ *Sound*
☐ *Weight*
☐ *Personal Motion*

388. You made an enemy wait.

389. You walked with somebody you liked.

390. You backed an unfriendly person up against a wall.

391. You wandered happily.

392. Somebody found you were warm.

393. You found it was all right to watch.

394. You discovered you were not weak.

395. You made an unfriendly person weep.

Can you recall a time when:

396. You did not care where he went.

397. You were happy to watch somebody go.

398. You physically compelled somebody to come.

399. You had a good opinion of a wife.

400. You had a good opinion of a husband.

401. You discovered it wasn't wrong.

402. You did something wrong and it turned out all right.

403. You were complimented on writing.

404. You made somebody yell.

405. Pleasant objects were against you.

406. You were glad an object was about.

407. Objects were all about you and you were happy.

☐ *Sight*
☐ *Smell*
☐ *Touch*
☐ *Color*
☐ *Tone*
☐ *External Motion*
☐ *Emotion*
☐ *Loudness*
☐ *Body Position*
☐ *Sound*
☐ *Weight*
☐ *Personal Motion*

Can you recall a time when:

408. You were glad an object was above you.

409. Somebody accepted an object you wanted to give.

410. One object accompanied another.

411. You acquired an object you wanted.

□ *Sight*
□ *Smell*
□ *Touch*
□ *Color*
□ *Tone*
□ *External Motion*
□ *Emotion*
□ *Loudness*
□ *Body Position*
□ *Sound*
□ *Weight*
□ *Personal Motion*

412. You got action out of objects.

413. Somebody admired something you had.

414. An object advanced you.

415. You found an object adorned you.

416. You discovered affection for something you had not known you liked.

417. You threw something away of which you were afraid.

418. You ran after an object and caught it.

419. Something aided you.

Can you recall a time when:

420. You were glad to get rid of all of something.

421. An object almost injured you but you were all right.

422. You attained an ambition for something.

423. You were among pleasant objects.

424. You found an animal was amiable.

425. You amused somebody with an object.

426. You were anxious about something and got rid of it.

427. A dangerous object approached and you got it away.

428. Somebody approved of something.

429. You arrested an object.

430. You were glad to be a rival of an object.

☐ *Sight*
☐ *Smell*
☐ *Touch*
☐ *Color*
☐ *Tone*
☐ *External Motion*
☐ *Emotion*
☐ *Loudness*
☐ *Body Position*
☐ *Sound*
☐ *Weight*
☐ *Personal Motion*

Can you recall a time when:

431. You were happy a car came.

432. You found you hadn't been ashamed without cause.

433. You put an animal to sleep.

434. You assailed something victoriously.

□ *Sight*
□ *Smell*
□ *Touch*
□ *Color*
□ *Tone*
□ *External Motion*
□ *Emotion*
□ *Loudness*
□ *Body Position*
□ *Sound*
□ *Weight*
□ *Personal Motion*

435. You assisted somebody with something.

436. You stopped associating with something you didn't like.

437. An object gave you assurance.

438. You astonished people with something.

439. You attacked something successfully.

440. You attracted an object.

441. You threw a ball up.

442. You considered something beautiful.

Can you recall a time when:

443. Somebody begged you for something.

444. You made a machine behave.

445. You were glad you were behind something.

446. You were happy to be below something.

447. You didn't believe in an object.

448. You were between two objects.

449. You blew something out.

450. You scraped bottom.

451. You acquired bread.

452. You polished an object.

453. You burned something you didn't want.

454. You buried something you disliked.

□ *Sight*
□ *Smell*
□ *Touch*
□ *Color*
□ *Tone*
□ *External Motion*
□ *Emotion*
□ *Loudness*
□ *Body Position*
□ *Sound*
□ *Weight*
□ *Personal Motion*

Can you recall a time when:

455. You captured something.

456. You did something skillful with a car.

457. You found out you didn't have to be careful with an object.

458. You were successfully careless.

□ *Sight*
□ *Smell*
□ *Touch*
□ *Color*
□ *Tone*
□ *External Motion*
□ *Emotion*
□ *Loudness*
□ *Body Position*
□ *Sound*
□ *Weight*
□ *Personal Motion*

459. You charmed somebody with something.

460. You became certain about something.

461. You took care of some possession because you wanted to.

462. You saw something coming in time.

463. You exerted your command over an object.

464. You concealed something.

465. You condemned an object.

466. You gave somebody something and it gave them confidence.

Can you recall a time when:

467. You resolved an object which had confounded you.

468. You conquered an object.

469. Something was given away with your consent.

470. You constructed something well.

471. You arranged something that was very convenient.

472. You showed courage about an object.

473. You cut something you didn't want.

474. You got rid of an unwanted object.

475. You delayed a physical action.

476. An item gave you delight.

477. You denied something existed.

478. You depended on an object.

☐ *Sight*
☐ *Smell*
☐ *Touch*
☐ *Color*
☐ *Tone*
☐ *External Motion*
☐ *Emotion*
☐ *Loudness*
☐ *Body Position*
☐ *Sound*
☐ *Weight*
☐ *Personal Motion*

Can you recall a time when:

479. You were happy to receive something you deserved.

480. You watched an unwanted object depart.

481. You took delight in destroying something.

☐ *Sight*
☐ *Smell*
☐ *Touch*
☐ *Color*
☐ *Tone*
☐ *External Motion*
☐ *Emotion*
☐ *Loudness*
☐ *Body Position*
☐ *Sound*
☐ *Weight*
☐ *Personal Motion*

482. You saw the difference between two objects.

483. You watched an object diminish.

484. You did something which others considered too difficult.

485. You were happy to dig.

486. You dispersed many objects.

487. You mastered something you distrusted.

488. You did what you pleased with something.

489. You understood an object you had doubted.

490. You drew something to you.

Can you recall a time when:

491. You gave an animal a drink.

492. You watched an object drop.

493. You dwelled in a pleasant place.

494. You waited eagerly.

495. Something looked too good to eat.

496. You succeeded in moving an object after a great deal of effort.

497. You enclosed an object.

498. Something encouraged you.

499. You made an end to an object.

☐ *Sight*
☐ *Smell*
☐ *Touch*
☐ *Color*
☐ *Tone*
☐ *External Motion*
☐ *Emotion*
☐ *Loudness*
☐ *Body Position*
☐ *Sound*
☐ *Weight*
☐ *Personal Motion*

500. You found an object considered an enemy was really a friend.

501. You enjoyed possessing something.

502. You felt you couldn't get enough of something.

503. You cut an entrance.

Can you recall a time when:

504. You escaped from an object.

505. You successfully examined something dangerous.

506. You were excited by something.

507. You exercised an animal.

□ *Sight*
□ *Smell*
□ *Touch*
□ *Color*
□ *Tone*
□ *External Motion*
□ *Emotion*
□ *Loudness*
□ *Body Position*
□ *Sound*
□ *Weight*
□ *Personal Motion*

508. You turned an object on its face.

509. An object was faithful.

510. You threw something far from you.

511. You made something go fast.

512. You overcame the fear of an object.

513. You fed an animal.

514. You took the first thing that came to you without qualms.

515. You made an object fit.

516. You watched somebody flee from an object and then approached it.

Can you recall a time when:

517. You owned something you had been forbidden to touch.

518. You successfully applied force.

519. You were proud of your possessions.

520. An object was a friend.

521. You frightened somebody with an object.

522. You happily gathered objects together.

523. You made something grow.

524. You were generous with objects.

525. You guarded something well.

526. An item made you very happy.

527. You were glad to do something harmful with an object.

528. You healed an animal.

☐ *Sight*
☐ *Smell*
☐ *Touch*
☐ *Color*
☐ *Tone*
☐ *External Motion*
☐ *Emotion*
☐ *Loudness*
☐ *Body Position*
☐ *Sound*
☐ *Weight*
☐ *Personal Motion*

Can you recall a time when:

529. You helped somebody with an object.

530. You found something somebody had hidden from you.

531. You hindered something bad.

532. You put a hole through an object.

□ *Sight*

□ *Smell*

□ *Touch*

□ *Color*

□ *Tone*

□ *External Motion*

□ *Emotion*

□ *Loudness*

□ *Body Position*

□ *Sound*

□ *Weight*

□ *Personal Motion*

533. You made an object very hot.

534. You hunted successfully.

535. You hurried to get something you wanted and achieved it.

536. You made an object hurt an enemy.

537. An object let you be idle.

538. You made something illuminate something.

539. You imagined a new object and made it.

540. You did the impossible with an object.

Can you recall a time when:

541. You watched something come in.

542. You increased your possessions.

543. Out of your own choice you took one object instead of another.

544. An object held your interest.

545. Somebody was happy with your invention.

546. You killed something bad.

547. You made an object jump.

548. You found that something was really yours.

549. You kissed an object out of happiness.

550. It was good that an object came too late.

551. You made somebody laugh with an object.

☐ *Sight*
☐ *Smell*
☐ *Touch*
☐ *Color*
☐ *Tone*
☐ *External Motion*
☐ *Emotion*
☐ *Loudness*
☐ *Body Position*
☐ *Sound*
☐ *Weight*
☐ *Personal Motion*

Can you recall a time when:

552. You took the length and breadth of an object.

553. You found an object lying.

554. You gave something life.

555. You lighted up a space well.

□ *Sight*
□ *Smell*
□ *Touch*
□ *Color*
□ *Tone*
□ *External Motion*
□ *Emotion*
□ *Loudness*
□ *Body Position*
□ *Sound*
□ *Weight*
□ *Personal Motion*

556. You were glad something was little.

557. You loved an object and kept it.

558. You managed a machine another couldn't manage.

559. You controlled an object.

560. You made an object make music.

561. You wrested a secret from some mysterious object.

562. You were glad to be mean to an object.

563. You mastered an intricate item.

Can you recall a time when:

564. You watched the meeting of two objects.

565. You threw fluid up into the air.

566. You heated a fluid.

567. You poured a fluid out.

568. You mixed two fluids.

569. You stirred a fluid.

570. You found something wasn't necessary.

571. You made an animal obey you.

572. You obliged somebody with an object.

573. You bought something for an occasion.

574. You shut up an object.

575. You organized a number of items well.

□ *Sight*
□ *Smell*
□ *Touch*
□ *Color*
□ *Tone*
□ *External Motion*
□ *Emotion*
□ *Loudness*
□ *Body Position*
□ *Sound*
□ *Weight*
□ *Personal Motion*

Can you recall a time when:

576. You discovered the origin of something.

577. You inflicted pain with an object and were glad to do so.

578. You put an object in your pocket.

☐ *Sight*
☐ *Smell*
☐ *Touch*
☐ *Color*
☐ *Tone*
☐ *External Motion*
☐ *Emotion*
☐ *Loudness*
☐ *Body Position*
☐ *Sound*
☐ *Weight*
☐ *Personal Motion*

579. An object made you feel rich.

580. You gave somebody something which was precious.

581. You prepared a mixture which was successful.

582. You preferred one object to the other.

583. You prevented harm from coming to an object.

584. You won a quarrel about an object.

585. You collected rain.

586. You acquired a fluid you wanted.

Can you recall a time when:

587. You raised an object.

588. You maintained something rare.

589. You were glad to receive something.

590. You recognized an object that puzzled others.

591. You gave an animal refuge.

592. You controlled an animal.

593. You restored an object.

594. You let somebody retain something valuable.

595. You made something run where others had failed.

596. You took an object to safety.

597. You put an object into something.

598. You took an object out of something.

☐ *Sight*
☐ *Smell*
☐ *Touch*
☐ *Color*
☐ *Tone*
☐ *External Motion*
☐ *Emotion*
☐ *Loudness*
☐ *Body Position*
☐ *Sound*
☐ *Weight*
☐ *Personal Motion*

Can you recall a time when:

599. You acquired something that was scarce.

600. You repaired a scratch on an object.

601. You made somebody scream with an object.

☐ *Sight*
☐ *Smell*
☐ *Touch*
☐ *Color*
☐ *Tone*
☐ *External Motion*
☐ *Emotion*
☐ *Loudness*
☐ *Body Position*
☐ *Sound*
☐ *Weight*
☐ *Personal Motion*

602. Someone found they had been too severe about an object.

603. You shook fluid off something.

604. You pulled an animal out of water.

605. You acquired an animal for food.

606. You tied an animal to a stake.

607. You struggled successfully with an object.

608. You stroked an object.

609. You were too strong for an object.

610. Something was submitted to you as a tribute.

Can you recall a time when:

611. People discovered you were to be congratulated about an object.

612. You handled an object well.

613. You seized an object.

614. Your search for an object was rewarded.

□ *Sight*
□ *Smell*
□ *Touch*
□ *Color*
□ *Tone*
□ *External Motion*
□ *Emotion*
□ *Loudness*
□ *Body Position*
□ *Sound*
□ *Weight*
□ *Personal Motion*

615. You were glad to see an object.

616. You maintained something.

617. You overcame something which had threatened you.

618. You stopped an object from being noisy.

619. You convinced someone of the value of an object.

620. You squandered some money.

621. You acquired some money.

622. You refused some money you didn't have coming.

Can you recall a time when:

623. You watched an unwanted object go.

624. You watched a desired object come.

625. You made something fly.

626. You left a space you didn't like.

☐ *Sight*
☐ *Smell*
☐ *Touch*
☐ *Color*
☐ *Tone*
☐ *External
    Motion*
☐ *Emotion*
☐ *Loudness*
☐ *Body
    Position*
☐ *Sound*
☐ *Weight*
☐ *Personal
    Motion*

627. You acquired a space you wanted.

628. You admired an area.

629. You advanced through space.

630. You felt affection for a space.

631. You were against a space.

632. You decorated a space.

633. You were glad to get out of a space of which you were afraid.

634. You aided in making space.

635. You were pleasantly alone in space.

Can you recall a time when:

636. You were in an amusing space.

637. You conquered a distance.

638. You got through an unwholesome space.

639. You arrived in a pleasant space.

640. You opened up a space.

641. You gave another assurance about a space.

642. You were attracted to a space.

643. You awakened in a pleasant place.

644. You burned off a space.

645. You blindly, but successfully, got through an area.

646. You enjoyed a black space.

647. You made a box.

648. You went into a pleasant place.

☐ *Sight*
☐ *Smell*
☐ *Touch*
☐ *Color*
☐ *Tone*
☐ *External Motion*
☐ *Emotion*
☐ *Loudness*
☐ *Body Position*
☐ *Sound*
☐ *Weight*
☐ *Personal Motion*

Can you recall a time when:

649. You took something out of a place.

650. You filled a place full.

651. You enjoyed a box.

652. You let a space be occupied.

☐ *Sight*
☐ *Smell*
☐ *Touch*
☐ *Color*
☐ *Tone*
☐ *External Motion*
☐ *Emotion*
☐ *Loudness*
☐ *Body Position*
☐ *Sound*
☐ *Weight*
☐ *Personal Motion*

653. You broke into a forbidden space.

654. You made a good cage.

655. You captured an area.

656. You took a child out of a place.

657. You straightened up a space.

658. You liked jumping through space.

659. You went below in space.

660. You made a broad space.

661. You collected many things in a place.

662. You created heat.

Can you recall a time when:

663. You brought a light.

664. You extinguished unfriendly energy.

665. You lit a light.

666. You regulated fire.

667. You successfully applied energy.

668. You burned something you didn't want.

669. You arranged lighting well.

670. You boiled something.

671. You made a machine run.

672. You dissipated heat.

673. You chilled something.

674. You went from a dark place into a friendly lighted one.

675. You were glad it was dark.

☐ *Sight*
☐ *Smell*
☐ *Touch*
☐ *Color*
☐ *Tone*
☐ *External Motion*
☐ *Emotion*
☐ *Loudness*
☐ *Body Position*
☐ *Sound*
☐ *Weight*
☐ *Personal Motion*

Can you recall a time when:

676. You left darkness behind you.

677. You were happy with the sunrise.

678. You watched twilight fade.

679. You saw lighted windows.

☐ *Sight*
☐ *Smell*
☐ *Touch*
☐ *Color*
☐ *Tone*
☐ *External Motion*
☐ *Emotion*
☐ *Loudness*
☐ *Body Position*
☐ *Sound*
☐ *Weight*
☐ *Personal Motion*

680. You found something with a light.

681. You were glad to enter a warm place.

682. You made a cold place warm.

683. You warmed somebody.

684. You heated something to eat.

685. You found companionship in fire.

686. You found somebody was warm against you.

687. You were glad to leave a cold place.

688. You made a barren place pleasant.

Can you recall a time when:

689. You found someone waiting for you in a dark place and were glad.

690. You regulated time well.

691. You left a bad time behind you.

692. You approached a good time.

693. You decided that things had not been so bad.

694. You found your time well spent.

695. You utilized some time yesterday.

696. You enjoyed a time today.

□ *Sight*
□ *Smell*
□ *Touch*
□ *Color*
□ *Tone*
□ *External Motion*
□ *Emotion*
□ *Loudness*
□ *Body Position*
□ *Sound*
□ *Weight*
□ *Personal Motion*

IMAGINATION

One of the most important parts of the thinking process is *imagination*. Imagination is actually a form of computation. Imagination gives calculated and instinctive solutions for the future. If an imagination is dulled, one's computation is seriously handicapped. Imagination is a good thing, not a bad thing. With daydreaming, for instance, a person can convert a not-too-pleasant existence into something livable. Only with imagination can one postulate future goals to attain.

If you take the word "imagination" apart, you will discover that it means merely the postulating of images or the assembly of perceptions into creations as you desire them. Imagination is something one does of his free will. Delusion could be said to be something forced upon one by his aberrations. All one has to know about imagination is know when he is imagining and when he is not.

Can you recall a time when:

1. You foresaw how something should be and so arranged it.

2. You imagined something and constructed it.

3. You envisioned how a place would look and went there.

☐ *Sight*
☐ *Smell*
☐ *Touch*
☐ *Color*
☐ *Tone*
☐ *External Motion*
☐ *Emotion*
☐ *Loudness*
☐ *Body Position*
☐ *Sound*
☐ *Weight*
☐ *Personal Motion*

4. You were forced to admit you lied when you had told the truth.

5. Somebody disarranged what was yours and you put it back.

6. You delighted in filling up space with imaginary things.

7. You did a masterpiece of creation.

8. You saw something come into actuality which you had imagined.

9. You imagined it was there and destroyed it.

10. Your vision was complimented.

Can you recall a time when:

11. You planned what to do with some time and did it.

12. You ignored interruptions and went on according to schedule.

13. You saw how some space could be bettered and bettered it.

14. You drew a plan and people followed it.

15. Things were smoother because you had thought of them that way.

16. You made profit out of imagination.

☐ *Sight*
☐ *Smell*
☐ *Touch*
☐ *Color*
☐ *Tone*
☐ *External Motion*
☐ *Emotion*
☐ *Loudness*
☐ *Body Position*
☐ *Sound*
☐ *Weight*
☐ *Personal Motion*

VALENCES

Y ou may have noticed, as you were perceiving things which have occurred in the past, that you were sometimes apparently inside your own body and sometimes may have been observing yourself. There are people who are never out of their own body in recall and people who are never in it. There are many *valences* in everyone. By a "valence" is meant an actual or a shadow personality. One's own valence is his actual personality. Be assured, however, he can get into a confusion with other bodies and persons. If one is in one's own valence when he is recalling things, he sees what he has seen just as though he were looking at it again with his own eyes. This is a very desirable condition of affairs. The symptom of being out of one's own valence and in a shadow valence might be said to mean that one finds his own body too dangerous to occupy in thought. Being out of valence makes perceptions hard to contact in recall. You will find as you continue these lists, repeating each one over and over, that it becomes easier and easier to see things again out of one's own eyes.

In the following list of questions and in any recall, one should make an effort to take the viewpoint of himself—which is to say, to see the scene and get the perceptions as he himself got them at the time.

Can you recall a time when:

1. You watched a person you didn't like doing something you liked to do.

2. You saw a person you liked doing something you didn't like to do.

3. You watched a person you liked doing something you liked to do.

□ *Sight*
□ *Smell*
□ *Touch*
□ *Color*
□ *Tone*
□ *External Motion*
□ *Emotion*
□ *Loudness*
□ *Body Position*
□ *Sound*
□ *Weight*
□ *Personal Motion*

4. You saw a person you disliked doing something you disliked to do.

5. You noticed somebody wearing something you wore.

6. You found somebody using a mannerism you used.

7. You adopted a mannerism.

8. You found yourself and a dog being treated alike.

9. You made faces at yourself in the mirror.

10. You decided to be completely different from a person.

Can you recall a time when:

11. You discovered you were like an object.

12. You were classified with an unfavorable person.

13. You were classified with a favorable person.

14. You found yourself dressed like many others.

15. You found you were different from somebody, after all.

16. You noticed the difference between yourself and others.

17. You ate with somebody you liked.

18. You met a person who reminded you of another and noticed the difference between them.

19. You walked in step with somebody you liked.

20. You rode with somebody you admired.

21. You had to take the same position as somebody else.

☐ *Sight*
☐ *Smell*
☐ *Touch*
☐ *Color*
☐ *Tone*
☐ *External Motion*
☐ *Emotion*
☐ *Loudness*
☐ *Body Position*
☐ *Sound*
☐ *Weight*
☐ *Personal Motion*

Can you recall a time when:

22. You played a game with people you liked.

23. You found yourself doing something because somebody in your early youth did it.

24. You found yourself refusing to do something because somebody in your early youth did it.

Note that the word "like" is used to mean admire or feel affection for and also to be similar to. The effort of valences could be said to mean trying to be like one's friends and unlike one's enemies. Unfortunately, in life one often has comparisons and similarities between himself and his enemies and has dissimilarities pointed out between himself and his friends. The adjustment of this is desirable so that one feels free to follow through any motion or action of any human being without associating the motion or action with either friend or enemy.

As an effort to straighten out one's associations and disassociations regarding people, the following questions are appended as the second part of List 9.

Recall:

1. A person who looks like you.

2. A person who has physical troubles similar to yours.

Recall:

3. **A person from whom you got a particular mannerism.**

4. **A person who reminds you of an animal you knew.**

5. **A person who compared you unfavorably to unfavorable persons.**

6. **A person who compared you favorably to favorable persons.**

7. **Two people whom you had confused with each other.**

8. **A person you knew long ago like a person you are living with.**

9. **A person whom you knew earlier who reminds you of a person with whom you are now connected.**

10. **Who you are most like? Who said so?**

11. **Who used to be afraid of sentiment?**

12. **Who didn't like to eat?**

13. **Who was never supposed to amount to anything?**

14. **Who associated with people too much?**

☐ *Sight*
☐ *Smell*
☐ *Touch*
☐ *Color*
☐ *Tone*
☐ *External Motion*
☐ *Emotion*
☐ *Loudness*
☐ *Body Position*
☐ *Sound*
☐ *Weight*
☐ *Personal Motion*

Recall:

15. Who made life miserable for everybody?

16. Who had bad manners?

☐ *Sight*
☐ *Smell*
☐ *Touch*
☐ *Color*
☐ *Tone*
☐ *External Motion*
☐ *Emotion*
☐ *Loudness*
☐ *Body Position*
☐ *Sound*
☐ *Weight*
☐ *Personal Motion*

17. Who did you know earlier that had the pain that bothers you?

18. Who would you most want to be like?

19. Who would you most hate to be like?

20. Who held that you amounted to nothing?

21. Who tried to keep you in line?

22. Who flattered you?

23. Who fed you?

It would be a good idea to go back over the last half of List 9 and recall specific incidents with all possible perceptions which illustrate the answers to these questions.

INTERRUPTIONS

 Slowness or uncertainty of speech, stage fright in part, slowness of computation—which is to say, thinking—and hesitancy in taking directions stem mainly from being *interrupted* in physical actions during early youth.

The child, because he may bring danger upon himself, is continually interrupted in his physical actions. He reaches for something and is turned away from it not simply by words, but by being himself removed from the object or having the object removed from him. He is kept out of spaces he wishes to enter by being pulled back. He is given one thing when he wants another. His self-determinism is thus continually interrupted in his efforts to explore, obtain or get rid of matter, energy, space or time. From these early interruptions, the child builds up a long chain of experiences of interruption not simply by speech, but by barriers and obstacles in the physical universe. If he has not been thoroughly interrupted when a child, he can analytically assess later interruptions. But if he has been handled and denied so as to interrupt him when he is young, his power of decision is inhibited—to say nothing of his power of speech and thought.

Recalling special incidents, as requested in this list, brings them into the light and takes the power from these chains of interruptions.

Can you recall a time when:

1. An object resisted you and you overcame it.

2. You couldn't move and then succeeded in getting away.

3. Somebody took something out of your hands and finished it.

□ *Sight*
□ *Smell*
□ *Touch*
□ *Color*
□ *Tone*
□ *External Motion*
□ *Emotion*
□ *Loudness*
□ *Body Position*
□ *Sound*
□ *Weight*
□ *Personal Motion*

4. Your physical action was interrupted.

5. A machine did not start.

6. Somebody jumped at you unexpectedly.

7. You were told a ghost story.

8. You had to give up a career.

9. Somebody touched your mouth.

10. You tried to raise your hand and were blocked.

11. You found the road was closed.

12. You couldn't get something into something.

Can you recall a time when:

13. You were halted by a friend.

14. Your father showed you how it was really done.

15. Somebody made you take care of something.

16. It was demonstrated you were putting it to the wrong use.

17. You were corrected "for your own good."

18. You knew somebody who had a mania for using only the right word.

19. You were "helped" by having your sentence finished.

20. You couldn't go at the last minute.

21. You knew somebody who corrected the words you used for songs.

22. You weren't permitted to cry.

23. Noise got on somebody's nerves.

☐ *Sight*
☐ *Smell*
☐ *Touch*
☐ *Color*
☐ *Tone*
☐ *External Motion*
☐ *Emotion*
☐ *Loudness*
☐ *Body Position*
☐ *Sound*
☐ *Weight*
☐ *Personal Motion*

Can you recall a time when:

24. You couldn't finish it for want of time.

25. You had to be patient.

26. You couldn't go just then.

27. You were going but you were stopped.

□ *Sight*
□ *Smell*
□ *Touch*
□ *Color*
□ *Tone*
□ *External Motion*
□ *Emotion*
□ *Loudness*
□ *Body Position*
□ *Sound*
□ *Weight*
□ *Personal Motion*

28. Somebody tried to stop you but you kept on anyway.

29. You used it just as you pleased.

30. You had not been halted.

31. You got loose and continued.

32. You yelled anyway.

33. You completed it despite somebody.

34. You had to stop bolting your food.

35. You drank all you pleased.

36. You weren't supposed to fight.

37. Somebody checked a muscular reaction.

Can you recall a time when:

38. You were very enthusiastic and somebody cooled it quickly.

39. You went on in spite of weariness.

40. You broke a habit.

41. You found somebody wasn't as strong as you had supposed.

42. You discovered you could have it after all.

43. You found the real motive was selfishness.

44. You got out from under domination.

45. You discovered it wasn't for your own good after all.

46. You stopped yourself from interrupting somebody.

47. You found other people weren't wiser than you.

48. Everybody thought you were wrong but discovered you had been right.

☐ *Sight*
☐ *Smell*
☐ *Touch*
☐ *Color*
☐ *Tone*
☐ *External Motion*
☐ *Emotion*
☐ *Loudness*
☐ *Body Position*
☐ *Sound*
☐ *Weight*
☐ *Personal Motion*

Can you recall a time when:

49. You attained the goal anyway.

50. You discovered another person wasn't worth having.

□ *Sight*
□ *Smell*
□ *Touch*
□ *Color*
□ *Tone*
□ *External Motion*
□ *Emotion*
□ *Loudness*
□ *Body Position*
□ *Sound*
□ *Weight*
□ *Personal Motion*

51. You restrained an urge to destroy something.

52. You disobeyed the law and got away with it.

53. Lightning didn't strike you.

54. You fixed something.

55. You ignored an interruption to your reading.

INVALIDATION SECTION

Aberrated individuals use two distinct and very aberrated methods of controlling others. The first consists of forcing the other person to do exactly what is desired with the mechanism of recrimination and denial of friendship or support unless instant compliance takes place. In other words, "You do exactly what I say or I am no ally of yours." This is outright *domination*. Additionally, it seeks by anger and outright criticism, accusations and other mechanisms to pound another individual into submission by making him less. The second method might be called domination by *nullification*. This is covert and quite often the person upon whom it is exerted remains unsuspecting beyond the fact that he knows he is very unhappy. This is the coward's method of domination. The person using it feels that he is less than the individual upon whom he is using it and has not the honesty or fortitude to admit the fact to himself. He then begins, much as termites gnaw away a foundation (as in California), to pull the other individual "down to size" using small carping criticisms. The one who is seeking to dominate strikes heavily at the point of pride and capability of his target. And yet, if at any moment the target challenges the nullifier, the person using the mechanism claims he is doing so solely out of assistance and friendship or disavows completely that it has been done.

Of the two methods, the latter is far more damaging. A person using this method seeks to reduce another individual down to a point where he can be completely controlled and will not stop until he has reduced the target into a confused apathy. The lowest common denominator of nullification could be called "invalidation." The nullifier seeks to invalidate not only the person, but the skills and knowledge of his target. The possessions of the target are said to be not quite as important as they might be. The experiences of the person being nullified are minimized. The target's looks, strength, physical capabilities and potentialities are also invalidated. All this may be done so covertly that it appears to be "in the best interest of" the target. The nullifier seeks to "improve" the person being invalidated.

The first question of this list should be, of course, how many people have you known who have sought consistently, under the mask of seeking to aid you, to tear you apart as a person and reduce your future, your hopes, your goals and the very energy of your life?

Can you recall a time when:

1. **A person much smaller than you resented your size.**

2. **A person bigger than you made you feel inferior.**

3. **A person would not let you finish something.**

4. **An object was too much for you.**

5. **You found a space too big.**

6. **You were pushed back because you were too small.**

7. **You didn't make the team.**

8. **You found you were adequate.**

9. **You found somebody had lied about how bad you were.**

10. **You discovered you had been right, after all.**

11. **You found your decision would have been best.**

☐ *Sight*
☐ *Smell*
☐ *Touch*
☐ *Color*
☐ *Tone*
☐ *External Motion*
☐ *Emotion*
☐ *Loudness*
☐ *Body Position*
☐ *Sound*
☐ *Weight*
☐ *Personal Motion*

Can you recall a time when:

12. You solved a problem nobody else could do.

13. You discovered there were homelier people in the world than you.

14. You found you could ignore somebody's opinion.

□ *Sight*
□ *Smell*
□ *Touch*
□ *Color*
□ *Tone*
□ *External Motion*
□ *Emotion*
□ *Loudness*
□ *Body Position*
□ *Sound*
□ *Weight*
□ *Personal Motion*

15. You found somebody else thought you really had done something good.

16. You were admired for your looks.

17. You overcame a machine.

18. You accomplished an arduous journey.

19. You discovered somebody who slurred you was dishonest in other ways.

20. You found you were bigger and more powerful than an animal.

21. You discovered your competence.

22. You bested somebody thoroughly.

Can you recall a time when:

23. An enemy cried for quarter.

24. You drew blood on somebody else.

25. You took the lion's share and kept it.

26. You made your weight felt.

27. You were too heavy for somebody.

□ *Sight*
□ *Smell*
□ *Touch*
□ *Color*
□ *Tone*
□ *External Motion*

28. You killed something.

29. You won.

□ *Emotion*
□ *Loudness*
□ *Body Position*
□ *Sound*
□ *Weight*
□ *Personal Motion*

30. You were able to get away from somebody who invalidated you.

31. You discovered you were right and the old man was wrong.

32. You found you could get better.

33. You got well when they had no hope for you.

34. You surprised yourself with your own endurance.

Can you recall a time when:

☐ *Sight*

☐ *Smell*

☐ *Touch*

☐ *Color*

☐ *Tone*

☐ *External Motion*

☐ *Emotion*

☐ *Loudness*

☐ *Body Position*

☐ *Sound*

☐ *Weight*

☐ *Personal Motion*

35. You discovered you did understand.

36. You did a job nobody believed possible.

37. You were proud of yourself today.

THE ELEMENTS

M an's primary foe in his environment is the weather. Houses, stoves, clothes and even food, in the degree that it furnishes body warmth and mobility, are weapons of defense against storm, cold, heat and night.

Can you recall a time when:

1. You bested a storm.

2. You enjoyed thunder.

3. You had fun in snow.

4. You enjoyed the sunshine.

5. Everyone else said it was too hot but you enjoyed it.

6. You bested an area of water.

7. The rain was soothing.

□ *Sight*
□ *Smell*
□ *Touch*
□ *Color*
□ *Tone*
□ *External Motion*
□ *Emotion*
□ *Loudness*
□ *Body Position*
□ *Sound*
□ *Weight*
□ *Personal Motion*

Can you recall a time when:

8. You were glad it was a cloudy day.

9. The wind excited you.

10. The night was soft.

11. You were glad to see the Sun.

☐ *Sight*
☐ *Smell*
☐ *Touch*
☐ *Color*
☐ *Tone*
☐ *External Motion*
☐ *Emotion*
☐ *Loudness*
☐ *Body Position*
☐ *Sound*
☐ *Weight*
☐ *Personal Motion*

12. The weather was friendly.

13. You bested some surf.

14. The air was exhilarating.

15. You were glad of the season.

16. You got warm after being too cold.

17. A dawn excited you.

18. You felt you owned the stars.

19. You were excited over a hailstone.

20. You discovered the pattern of snowflakes.

21. The dew was bright.

Can you recall a time when:

22. A soft fog rolled.

23. You won over a storm's violence.

24. It was terrible outside and you were snug in your house.

25. The wind felt good.

26. You lived through it.

27. You discovered you liked your own climate.

28. You were glad to see spring.

29. You felt you could best the winds of the world.

30. You admired a storm.

31. You enjoyed lightning.

□ *Sight*
□ *Smell*
□ *Touch*
□ *Color*
□ *Tone*
□ *External Motion*
□ *Emotion*
□ *Loudness*
□ *Body Position*
□ *Sound*
□ *Weight*
□ *Personal Motion*

BEGIN AT LIST 1 AGAIN AND GO THROUGH ALL LISTS ONCE MORE UNTIL BOOK HAS BEEN USED MANY TIMES.

If Recalling a Certain Thing Made You Uncomfortable

 It may be, as you recall certain incidents in your life, that you are rendered uncomfortable. There are several ways of overcoming this.

PHYSICAL PAIN:

If actual *physical pain* is part of the situation you have recalled, do not try to force yourself further into it, but concentrate on later incidents which gradually get you back up to present time. These questions will assist you to do that.

1. Recall a pleasant incident which happened later.

2. Recall what you were doing this time last year.

3. Recall a moment when you were really enjoying yourself.

4. Recall what you were doing this time last month.

5. Recall what you were doing yesterday.

6. Recall something pleasant that happened today.

Recall all these things consecutively once again.

SORROW:

If no physical pain was included, but *sorrow* was, recall the following:

1. The next time after that you acquired something you liked.

2. Recall something you have now which you enjoy.

3. Recall something you wanted a long time and finally got.

4. Recall the time somebody was very nice to you.

5. Recall the last money you got.

6. Recall eating dinner last night.

7. Recall eating today.

☐ *Sight*
☐ *Smell*
☐ *Touch*
☐ *Color*
☐ *Tone*
☐ *External Motion*
☐ *Emotion*
☐ *Loudness*
☐ *Body Position*
☐ *Sound*
☐ *Weight*
☐ *Personal Motion*

Recall all of these incidents over again with all available perceptics.

If you consistently hit physical pain and grief incidents in your processing and do not seem to be able to do anything about it, call your local Dianetic auditor and arrange a professional visit so that you can be brought up to a point where the list is a benefit.

WANTING TO AVOID RECOLLECTIONS:

If you merely became uncomfortable without great sorrow or physical pain, but simply wanted to *avoid the recollection,* use the following list:

1. Recall the incident again in its entirety from first to last.

2. Recall the incident once more.

3. Recall an earlier incident similar to it.

4. Recall an even earlier incident similar to it.

☐ *Sight*
☐ *Smell*
☐ *Touch*
☐ *Color*
☐ *Tone*
☐ *External Motion*
☐ *Emotion*
☐ *Loudness*
☐ *Body Position*
☐ *Sound*
☐ *Weight*
☐ *Personal Motion*

5. Recall the earliest incident that you can get like it.

6. Recall all these incidents, one after the other, in their entirety.

7. Recall all the incidents again, one after the other, from the earliest to the latest.

8. Recall all these incidents again.

9. Go over the chain of similar incidents and find later ones on up to present time.

10. Recall a pleasant incident which has happened in the last few days. Get all possible perceptics on it.

11. Recall what you were doing an hour ago.

STABILIZATION:

This usually stabilizes *any* of the above conditions.

1. **Recall a time which really seems real to you.**

2. **Recall a time when you felt real affinity from someone.**

3. **Recall a time when someone was in good communication with you.**

4. **Recall a time when you felt deep affinity for somebody else.**

5. **Recall a time when you knew you were really communicating to somebody.**

6. **Recall a time when several people agreed with you completely.**

7. **Recall a time when you were in agreement with somebody else.**

8. **Recall a time within the last two days when you felt affectionate.**

9. **Recall a time in the last two days when somebody felt affection for you.**

10. **Recall a time in the last two days when you were in good communication with someone.**

11. Recall a time in the last two days which really seems real to you.

12. Recall a time in the last two days when you were in good communication with people.

Recall several incidents of each kind.

According to the practice of medicine and after experiment, it has been found that B_1 is necessary in large amounts during processing. A good protein diet and some 100 to 200 mg per day of B_1 have been found to materially assist processing. Failure to take B_1 and to use a heavy protein diet have been found to result in nightmares and nervousness when one is undergoing processing. Note that this is a medical finding dating back many years and is not original with Dianetics.

END OF SESSION LIST

E ach time you give yourself a session of processing, you should finish off with the following routine without disk.

1. **Rapidly sketch over the session just ended.**

2. **Sketch over what you have been doing again, with particular attention to how you have been sitting.**

3. **Go over the period of the session with regard only to what you have been doing with your hands and things in the exterior world you have heard during this session.**

4. **Fix your attention upon a pleasant object near you now.**

Repeat this until you feel refreshed in your immediate surroundings.

APPENDIX

FURTHER STUDY
BOOKS & LECTURES BY L. RON HUBBARD

The materials of Dianetics and Scientology comprise the largest body of information ever assembled on the mind, spirit and life, rigorously refined and codified by L. Ron Hubbard through five decades of research, investigation and development. The results of that work are contained in hundreds of books and more than 3,000 recorded lectures. A full listing and description of them all can be obtained from any Scientology Church or Publications Organization. (See *Guide to the Materials.*)

The books and lectures below form the foundation upon which the Bridge to Freedom is built. They are listed in the sequence Ron wrote or delivered them. In many instances, Ron gave a series of lectures immediately following the release of a new book to provide further explanation and insight of these milestones. Through monumental restoration efforts, those lectures are now available and are listed herein with their companion book.

While Ron's books contain the summaries of breakthroughs and conclusions as they appeared in the developmental research track, his lectures provide the running day-to-day record of research and explain the thoughts, conclusions, tests and demonstrations that lay along that route. In that regard, they are the complete record of the entire research track, providing not only the most important breakthroughs in Man's history, but the *why* and *how* Ron arrived at them.

Not the least advantage of a chronological study of these books and lectures is the inclusion of words and terms which, when originally used, were defined by LRH with considerable exactitude. Far beyond a mere "definition," entire lectures are devoted to a full description of each new Dianetic or Scientology term—what made the breakthrough possible, its application in auditing as well as its application to life itself. As a result, one leaves behind no misunderstoods, obtains a full conceptual understanding of Dianetics and Scientology and grasps the subjects at a level not otherwise possible.

Through a sequential study, you can see how the subject progressed and recognize the highest levels of development. The listing of books and lectures below shows where *Self Analysis* fits within the developmental line. From there you can determine your *next* step or any earlier books and lectures you may have missed. You will then be able to fill in missing gaps, not only gaining knowledge of each breakthrough, but greater understanding of what you've already studied.

This is the path to knowing how to know, unlocking the gates to your future eternity. Follow it.

DIANETICS: THE ORIGINAL THESIS • Ron's *first* description of Dianetics. Originally circulated in manuscript form, it was soon copied and passed from hand to hand. Ensuing word of mouth created such demand for more information, Ron concluded the only way to answer the inquiries was with a book. That book was Dianetics: The Modern Science of Mental Health, now the all-time self-help bestseller. Find out what started it all. For here is the bedrock foundation of Dianetic discoveries: the *Original Axioms*, the *Dynamic Principle of Existence*, the *Anatomy of the Analytical* and *Reactive Mind*, the *Dynamics*, the *Tone Scale*, the *Auditor's Code* and the first description of a *Clear*. Even more than that, here are the primary laws describing *how* and *why* auditing works. It's only here in Dianetics: The Original Thesis.

DIANETICS: THE EVOLUTION OF A SCIENCE • This is the story of *how* Ron discovered the reactive mind and developed the procedures to get rid of it. Originally written for a national magazine—published to coincide with the release of Dianetics: The Modern Science of Mental Health—it started a wildfire movement virtually overnight upon that book's publication. Here then are both the fundamentals of Dianetics as well as the only account of Ron's two-decade journey of discovery and how he applied a scientific methodology to the problems of the human mind. He wrote it so you would know. Hence, this book is a must for every Dianeticist and Scientologist.

DIANETICS: THE MODERN SCIENCE OF MENTAL HEALTH • The bolt from the blue that began a worldwide movement. For while Ron had previously announced his discovery of the reactive mind, it had only fueled the fire of those wanting more information. More to the point—it was humanly impossible for one man to clear an entire planet. Encompassing all his previous discoveries and case histories of those breakthroughs in application, Ron provided the complete handbook of Dianetics procedure to train auditors to use it everywhere. A bestseller for more than half a century and with tens of millions of copies in print, Dianetics: The Modern Science of Mental Health has been translated in more than fifty languages, and used in more than 100 countries of Earth—indisputably, the most widely read and influential book about the human mind ever written. And that is why it will forever be known as *Book One*.

DIANETICS LECTURES AND DEMONSTRATIONS • Immediately following the publication of *Dianetics*, LRH began lecturing to packed auditoriums across America. Although addressing thousands at a time, demand continued to grow. To meet that demand, his presentation in Oakland, California, was recorded. In these four lectures, Ron related the events that sparked his investigation and his personal journey to his groundbreaking discoveries. He followed it all with a personal demonstration of Dianetics auditing—the only such demonstration of Book One available. *4 lectures.*

DIANETICS PROFESSIONAL COURSE LECTURES—*A SPECIAL COURSE FOR BOOK ONE AUDITORS* • Following six months of coast-to-coast travel, lecturing to the first Dianeticists, Ron assembled auditors in Los Angeles for a new Professional Course. The subject was his next sweeping discovery on life—the *ARC Triangle,* describing the interrelationship of *Affinity, Reality* and *Communication.* Through a series of fifteen lectures, LRH announced many firsts, including the *Spectrum of Logic,* containing an infinity of gradients from right to wrong; *ARC and the Dynamics;* the *Tone Scales of ARC;* the *Auditor's Code* and how it relates to ARC; and the *Accessibility Chart* that classifies a case and how to process it. Here, then, is both the final statement on Book One Auditing Procedures and the discovery upon which all further research would advance. The data in these lectures was thought to be lost for over fifty years and only available in student notes published in Notes on the Lectures. The original recordings have now been discovered making them broadly available for the first time. Life in its highest state, *Understanding,* is composed of Affinity, Reality and Communication. And, as LRH said, the best description of the ARC Triangle to be found anywhere is in these lectures. *15 lectures.*

SCIENCE OF SURVIVAL—*PREDICTION OF HUMAN BEHAVIOR* • The most useful book you will ever own. Built around the *Hubbard Chart of Human Evaluation,* Science of Survival provides the first accurate prediction of human behavior. Included on the chart are all the manifestations of an individual's survival potential graduated from highest to lowest, making this the complete book on the Tone Scale. Knowing only one or two characteristics of a person and using this chart, you can plot his or her position on the Tone Scale and thereby know the rest, obtaining an accurate index of their *entire* personality, conduct and character. Before this book the world was convinced that cases could not improve but only deteriorate. Science of Survival presents the idea of different states of case and the brand-new idea that one can progress upward on the Tone Scale. And therein lies the basis of today's Grade Chart.

THE SCIENCE OF SURVIVAL LECTURES • Underlying the development of the Tone Scale and Chart of Human Evaluation was a monumental breakthrough: The *Theta-MEST Theory,* containing the explanation of the interaction between Life—*theta*—with the physical universe of Matter, Energy, Space and Time—*MEST.* In these lectures, delivered to students immediately following publication of the book, Ron gave the most expansive description of all that lies behind the Chart of Human Evaluation and its application in life itself. Moreover, here also is the explanation of how the ratio of *theta* and *en(turbulated)-theta* determines one's position on the Tone Scale and the means to ascend to higher states. *4 lectures.*

SELF ANALYSIS • *(This current volume.)* The barriers of life are really just shadows. Learn to know yourself—not just a shadow of yourself. Containing the most complete description of consciousness, Self Analysis takes you through your past, through your potentials, your life. First, with a series of self-examinations and using a special version of the Hubbard Chart of Human Evaluation, you plot yourself on the Tone Scale. Then, applying a series of light yet powerful processes, you embark on the great adventure of self-discovery. This book further contains embracive principles that reach *any* case, from the lowest to the highest—including auditing techniques so effective they are referred to by Ron again and again through all following years of research into the highest states. In sum, this book not only moves one up the Tone Scale but can pull a person out of almost anything.

ADVANCED PROCEDURE AND AXIOMS • With new breakthroughs on the nature and anatomy of engrams—"Engrams are effective only when the individual himself determines that they will be effective"—came the discovery of the being's use of a *Service Facsimile:* a mechanism employed to explain away failures in life, but which then locks a person into detrimental patterns of behavior and further failure. In consequence came a new type of processing addressing *Thought, Emotion* and *Effort* detailed in the "Fifteen Acts" of Advanced Procedure and oriented to the rehabilitation of the preclear's *Self-determinism.* Hence, this book also contains the all-encompassing, no-excuses-allowed explanation of *Full Responsibility,* the key to unlocking it all. Moreover, here is the codification of *Definitions, Logics,* and *Axioms,* providing both the summation of the entire subject and direction for all future research. *See Handbook for Preclears, written as a companion self-processing manual to Advanced Procedure and Axioms.*

THOUGHT, EMOTION AND EFFORT • With the codification of the Axioms came the means to address key points on a case that could unravel all aberration. *Basic Postulates, Prime Thought, Cause and Effect* and their effect on everything from *memory* and *responsibility* to an individual's own role in empowering *engrams*—these matters are only addressed in this series. Here, too, is the most complete description of the *Service Facsimile* found anywhere—and why its resolution removes an individual's self-imposed disabilities. *21 lectures.*

HANDBOOK FOR PRECLEARS • The "Fifteen Acts" of Advanced Procedure and Axioms are paralleled by the fifteen Self-processing Acts given in Handbook for Preclears. Moreover, this book contains several essays giving the most expansive description of the *Ideal State of Man*. Discover why behavior patterns become so solidly fixed; why habits seemingly can't be broken; how decisions long ago have more power over a person than his decisions today; and why a person keeps past negative experiences in the present. It's all clearly laid out on the Chart of Attitudes—a milestone breakthrough that complements the Chart of Human Evaluation—plotting the ideal state of being and one's *attitudes* and *reactions* to life. *In self-processing, Handbook for Preclears is used in conjunction with Self Analysis.*

THE LIFE CONTINUUM • Besieged with requests for lectures on his latest breakthroughs, Ron replied with everything they wanted and more at the Second Annual Conference of Dianetic Auditors. Describing the technology that lies behind the self-processing steps of the *Handbook*—here is the *how* and *why* of it all: the discovery of *Life Continuum*—the mechanism by which an individual is compelled to carry on the life of another deceased or departed individual, generating in his own body the infirmities and mannerisms of the departed. Combined with auditor instruction on use of the Chart of Attitudes in determining how to enter every case at the proper gradient, here, too, are directions for dissemination of the Handbook and hence, the means to begin wide-scale clearing. *10 lectures.*

SCIENTOLOGY: MILESTONE ONE • Ron began the first lecture in this series with six words that would change the world forever: "This is a course in *Scientology.*" From there, Ron not only described the vast scope of this, a then brand-new subject, he also detailed his discoveries on past lives. He proceeded from there to the description of the first E-Meter and its initial use in uncovering the *theta line* (the entire track of a thetan's existence), as entirely distinct from the *genetic body line* (the time track of bodies and their physical evolution), shattering the "one-life" lie and revealing the *whole track* of spiritual existence. Here, then, is the very genesis of Scientology. *22 lectures.*

THE ROUTE TO INFINITY: TECHNIQUE 80 LECTURES • As Ron explained, "Technique 80 is the *To Be or Not To Be* Technique." With that, he unveiled the crucial foundation on which ability and sanity rest: *the being's capacity to make a decision.* Here, then, is the anatomy of "maybe," the *Wavelengths of ARC*, the *Tone Scale of Decisions*, and the means to rehabilitate a being's ability *To Be...*almost *anything. 7 lectures.* *(Knowledge of Technique 80 is required for Technique 88 as described in Scientology: A History of Man—below.)*

SCIENTOLOGY: A HISTORY OF MAN • "A cold-blooded and factual account of your last 76 trillion years." So begins A History of Man, announcing the revolutionary *Technique 88*—revealing for the first time the truth about whole track experience and the exclusive address, in auditing, to the thetan. Here is history unraveled with the first E-Meter, delineating and describing the principal incidents on the whole track to be found in any human being: *Electronic implants, entities,* the *genetic track, between-lives incidents, how bodies evolved* and *why you got trapped in them*—they're all detailed here.

    TECHNIQUE 88: INCIDENTS ON THE TRACK BEFORE EARTH • "Technique 88 is the most hyperbolical, effervescent, dramatic, unexaggeratable, high-flown, superlative, grandiose, colossal and magnificent technique which the mind of Man could conceivably embrace. It is as big as the whole track and all the incidents on it. It's what you apply it to; it's what's been going on. It contains the riddles and secrets, the mysteries of all time. You could bannerline this technique like they do a sideshow, but nothing you could say, no adjective you could use, would adequately describe even a small segment of it. It not only batters the imagination, it makes you ashamed to imagine anything," is Ron's introduction to you in this never-before-available lecture series, expanding on all else contained in History of Man. What awaits you is the whole track itself. *15 lectures.*

SCIENTOLOGY 8-80 • The *first* explanation of the electronics of human thought and the energy phenomena in any being. Discover how even physical universe laws of motion are mirrored in a being, not to mention the electronics of aberration. Here is the link between theta and MEST revealing what energy *is*, and how you *create* it. It was this breakthrough that revealed the subject of a thetan's *flows* and which, in turn, is applied in *every* auditing process today. In the book's title, "8-8" stands for *Infinity-Infinity,* and "0" represents the static, *theta.* Included are the *Wavelengths of Emotion, Aesthetics, Beauty and Ugliness, Inflow and Outflow* and the *Sub-zero Tone Scale*—applicable only to the thetan.

    SOURCE OF LIFE ENERGY • Beginning with the announcement of his new book—Scientology 8-80—Ron not only unveiled his breakthroughs of theta as the Source of Life Energy, but detailed the *Methods of Research* he used to make that and every other discovery of Dianetics and Scientology: the Qs and *Logics*—methods of *thinking* applicable to any universe or thinking process. Here, then, is both *how to think* and *how to evaluate all data and knowledge,* and thus, the linchpin to a full understanding of both Scientology and life itself. *14 lectures.*

THE COMMAND OF THETA • While in preparation of his newest book and the Doctorate Course he was about to deliver, Ron called together auditors for a new Professional Course. As he said, "For the first time with this class we are stepping, really, beyond the scope of the word *Survival*." From that vantage point, the Command of Theta gives the technology that bridges the knowledge from 8-80 to 8-8008, and provides the first full explanation of the subject of *Cause* and a permanent shift of orientation in life from MEST to *Theta*. *10 lectures.*

SCIENTOLOGY 8-8008 • The complete description of the behavior and potentials of a *thetan*, and textbook for the Philadelphia Doctorate Course and The Factors: Admiration and the Renaissance of Beingness lectures. As Ron said, the book's title serves to fix in the mind of the individual a route by which he can rehabilitate himself, his abilities, his ethics and his goals—the attainment of *infinity* (8) by the reduction of the apparent *infinity* (8) of the MEST universe to *zero* (0) and the increase of the apparent *zero* (0) of one's own universe to *infinity* (8). Condensed herein are more than 80,000 hours of investigation, with a summarization and amplification of every breakthrough to date—and the full significance of those discoveries form the new vantage point of *Operating Thetan*.

THE PHILADELPHIA DOCTORATE COURSE LECTURES • This renowned series stands as the largest single body of work on the anatomy, behavior and potentials of the spirit of Man ever assembled, providing the very fundamentals which underlie the route to Operating Thetan. Here it is in complete detail—the thetan's relationship to the *creation, maintenance* and *destruction of universes*. In just those terms, here is the *anatomy* of matter, energy, space and time, and *postulating* universes into existence. Here, too, is the thetan's fall from whole track abilities and the *universal laws* by which they are restored. In short, here is Ron's codification of the upper echelon of theta beingness and behavior. Lecture after lecture fully expands every concept of the course text, Scientology 8-8008, providing the total scope of *you* in native state. *76 lectures and accompanying reproductions of the original 54 LRH hand-drawn lecture charts.*

THE FACTORS: ADMIRATION AND THE RENAISSANCE OF BEINGNESS • With the *potentials* of a thetan fully established came a look outward resulting in Ron's monumental discovery of a *universal solvent* and the basic laws of the theta *universe*—laws quite literally senior to anything: *The Factors: Summation of the Considerations of the Human Spirit and Material Universe*. So dramatic were these breakthroughs, Ron expanded the book Scientology 8-8008, both clarifying previous discoveries and adding chapter after chapter which, studied with these lectures, provide a postgraduate level to the Doctorate Course. Here then are lectures containing the knowledge of *universal truth* unlocking the riddle of creation itself. *18 lectures.*

THE CREATION OF HUMAN ABILITY—*A HANDBOOK FOR SCIENTOLOGISTS* •
On the heels of his discoveries of Operating Thetan came a year of intensive research, exploring the realm of a *thetan exterior*. Through auditing and instruction, including 450 lectures in this same twelve-month span, Ron codified the entire subject of Scientology. And it's all contained in this handbook, from a *Summary of Scientology* to its basic *Axioms* and *Codes*. Moreover, here is *Intensive Procedure*, containing the famed Exteriorization Processes of *Route 1* and *Route 2*—processes drawn right from the Axioms. Each one is described in detail—*how* the process is used, *why* it works, the axiomatic technology that underlies its use, and the complete explanation of how a being can break the *false agreements* and *self-created barriers* that enslave him to the physical universe. In short, this book contains the ultimate summary of thetan exterior OT ability and its permanent accomplishment.

 PHOENIX LECTURES: FREEING THE HUMAN SPIRIT • Here is the panoramic view of Scientology complete. Having codified the subject of Scientology in Creation of Human Ability, Ron then delivered a series of half-hour lectures to specifically accompany a full study of the book. From the *essentials* that underlie the technology—*The Axioms, Conditions of Existence* and *Considerations and Mechanics,* to the processes of *Intensive Procedure,* including twelve lectures describing one-by-one the thetan exterior processes of *Route 1*—it's all covered in full, providing a conceptual understanding of the *science of knowledge* and *native state OT ability*. Here then are the bedrock principles upon which everything in Scientology rests, including the embracive statement of the religion and its heritage—*Scientology, Its General Background*. Hence, this is the watershed lecture series on Scientology itself, and the axiomatic foundation for all future research. *42 lectures.*

DIANETICS 55!—*THE COMPLETE MANUAL OF HUMAN COMMUNICATION* •
With all breakthroughs to date, a single factor had been isolated as crucial to success in every type of auditing. As LRH said, "Communication is so thoroughly important today in Dianetics and Scientology (as it always has been on the whole track) that it could be said if you were to get a preclear into communication, you would get him well." And this book delineates the *exact,* but previously unknown, anatomy and formulas for *perfect* communication. The magic of the communication cycle is *the* fundamental of auditing and the primary reason auditing works. The breakthroughs here opened new vistas of application—discoveries of such magnitude, LRH called Dianetics 55! the *Second Book* of Dianetics.

THE UNIFICATION CONGRESS: COMMUNICATION! FREEDOM & ABILITY • The historic Congress announcing the reunification of the subjects of Dianetics and Scientology with the release of *Dianetics 55!* Until now, each had operated in their own sphere: Dianetics addressed Man *as Man*—the first four dynamics, while Scientology addressed *life itself*—the Fifth to Eighth Dynamics. The formula which would serve as the foundation for all future development was contained in a single word: *Communication*. It was a paramount breakthrough Ron would later call, "the great discovery of Dianetics and Scientology." Here, then, are the lectures, as it happened. *16 lectures and accompanying reproductions of the original LRH hand-drawn lecture charts.*

SCIENTOLOGY: THE FUNDAMENTALS OF THOUGHT—*THE BASIC BOOK OF THE THEORY AND PRACTICE OF SCIENTOLOGY FOR BEGINNERS* • Designated by Ron as the *Book One of Scientology*. After having fully unified and codified the subjects of Dianetics and Scientology came the refinement of their *fundamentals*. Originally published as a résumé of Scientology for use in translations into non-English tongues, this book is of inestimable value to both the beginner and advanced student of the mind, spirit and life. Equipped with this book alone, one can begin a practice and perform seeming miracle changes in the states of well-being, ability and intelligence of people. Contained within are the *Conditions of Existence, Eight Dynamics, ARC Triangle, Parts of Man*, the full analysis of *Life as a Game*, and more, including exact processes for individual application of these principles in processing. Here, then, in one book, is the starting point for bringing Scientology to people everywhere.

 HUBBARD PROFESSIONAL COURSE LECTURES • While Fundamentals of Thought stands as an introduction to the subject for beginners, it also contains a distillation of fundamentals for every Scientologist. Here are the in-depth descriptions of those fundamentals, each lecture one-half hour in length and providing, one-by-one, a complete mastery of a single Scientology breakthrough—*Axioms 1-10; The Anatomy of Control; Handling of Problems; Start, Change and Stop; Confusion and Stable Data; Exteriorization; Valences* and more—the *why* behind them, *how* they came to be and their mechanics. And it's all brought together with the *Code of a Scientologist*, point by point, and its use in actually creating a new civilization. In short, here are the LRH lectures that make a *Professional Scientologist*—one who can apply the subject to every aspect of life. *21 lectures.*

ADDITIONAL BOOKS CONTAINING SCIENTOLOGY ESSENTIALS

WORK

THE PROBLEMS OF WORK—*SCIENTOLOGY APPLIED TO THE WORKADAY WORLD* • Having codified the entire subject of Scientology, Ron immediately set out to provide the *beginning* manual for its application by anyone. As he described it: life is composed of seven-tenths work, one-tenth familial, one-tenth political and one-tenth relaxation. Here, then, is Scientology applied to that seven-tenths of existence including the answers to *Exhaustion* and the *Secret of Efficiency*. Here, too, is the analysis of life itself—a game composed of exact rules. Know them and you succeed. Problems of Work contains technology no one can live without, and that can immediately be applied by both the Scientologist and those new to the subject.

LIFE PRINCIPLES

SCIENTOLOGY: A NEW SLANT ON LIFE • Scientology essentials for every aspect of life. Basic answers that put you in charge of your existence, truths to consult again and again: *Is It Possible to Be Happy?*, *Two Rules for Happy Living*, *Personal Integrity*, *The Anti-Social Personality* and many more. In every part of this book you will find Scientology truths that describe conditions in your life and furnish *exact* ways to improve them. Scientology: A New Slant on Life contains essential knowledge for every Scientologist and a perfect introduction for anyone new to the subject.

AXIOMS, CODES AND SCALES

SCIENTOLOGY 0-8: THE BOOK OF BASICS • The companion to *all* Ron's books, lectures and materials. This is *the* Book of Basics, containing indispensable data you will refer to constantly: the *Axioms of Dianetics and Scientology; The Factors;* a full compilation of all *Scales*—more than 100 in all; listings of the *Perceptics* and *Awareness Levels;* all *Codes* and *Creeds* and much more. The senior laws of existence are condensed into this single volume, distilled from more than 15,000 pages of writings, 3,000 lectures and scores of books.

SCIENTOLOGY ETHICS:
TECHNOLOGY OF OPTIMUM SURVIVAL

INTRODUCTION TO SCIENTOLOGY ETHICS • A new hope for Man arises with the first workable technology of ethics—technology to help an individual pull himself out of the downward skid of life and to a higher plateau of survival. This is the comprehensive handbook providing the crucial fundamentals: *Basics of Ethics & Justice; Honesty; Conditions of Existence; Condition Formulas* from Confusion to Power; the *Basics of Suppression* and its handling; as well as *Justice Procedures* and their use in Scientology Churches. Here, then, is the technology to overcome any barriers in life and in one's personal journey up the Bridge to Total Freedom.

PURIFICATION

CLEAR BODY, CLEAR MIND—*THE EFFECTIVE PURIFICATION PROGRAM* • We live in a biochemical world, and this book is the solution. While investigating the harmful effects that earlier drug use had on preclears' cases, Ron made the major discovery that many street drugs, particularly LSD, remained in a person's body long after ingested. Residues of the drug, he noted, could have serious and lasting effects, including triggering further "trips." Additional research revealed that a wide range of substances—medical drugs, alcohol, pollutants, household chemicals and even food preservatives—could also lodge in the body's tissues. Through research on thousands of cases, he developed the *Purification Program* to eliminate their destructive effects. Clear Body, Clear Mind details every aspect of the all-natural regimen that can free one from the harmful effects of drugs and other toxins, opening the way for spiritual progress.

REFERENCE HANDBOOKS

WHAT IS SCIENTOLOGY?

The complete and essential encyclopedic reference on the subject and practice of Scientology. Organized for use, this book contains the pertinent data on every aspect of the subject:

• The life of L. Ron Hubbard and his path of discovery

• The Spiritual Heritage of the religion

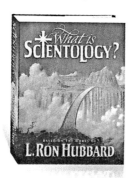

• A full description of Dianetics and Scientology

• Auditing—what it is and how it works

• Courses—what they contain and how they are structured

• The Grade Chart of Services and how one ascends to higher states

• The Scientology Ethics and Justice System

• The Organizational Structure of the Church

• A complete description of the many Social Betterment programs supported by the Church, including: Drug Rehabilitation, Criminal Reform, Literacy and Education and the instilling of real values for morality

Over 1,000 pages in length, with more than 500 photographs and illustrations, this text further includes Creeds, Codes, a full listing of all books and materials as well as a Catechism with answers to virtually any question regarding the subject.

You Ask and This Book Answers.

THE SCIENTOLOGY HANDBOOK

Scientology fundamentals for daily use in every part of life. Encompassing 19 separate bodies of technology, here is the most comprehensive manual on the basics of life ever published. Each chapter contains key principles and technology for your continual use:

• Study Technology

• The Dynamics of Existence

• The Components of Understanding— Affinity, Reality and Communication

• The Tone Scale

• Communication and its Formulas

• Assists for Illnesses and Injuries

• How to Resolve Conflicts

• Integrity and Honesty

• Ethics and Condition Formulas

• Answers to Suppression and a Dangerous Environment

• Marriage

• Children

• Tools for the Workplace

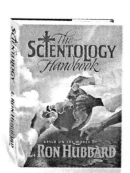

More than 700 photographs and illustrations make it easy for you to learn the procedures and apply them at once. This book is truly the indispensable handbook for every Scientologist.

The Technology to Build a Better World.

ABOUT L. RON HUBBARD

"To really know life," L. Ron Hubbard wrote, "you've got to be part of life. You must get down and look, you must get into the nooks and crannies of existence. You have to rub elbows with all kinds and types of men before you can finally establish what he is."

Through his long and extraordinary journey to the founding of Dianetics and Scientology, Ron did just that. From his adventurous youth in a rough and tumble American West to his far-flung trek across a still mysterious Asia; from his two-decade search for the very essence of life to the triumph of Dianetics and Scientology—such are the stories recounted in the L. Ron Hubbard Biographical Publications.

Presenting the photographic overview of Ron's greater journey is *L. Ron Hubbard: Images of a Lifetime*. Drawn from his own archival collection, this is Ron's life as he himself saw it.

While for the many aspects of that rich and varied life, stands the Ron Series. Each issue focuses on a specific LRH profession: *Auditor, Humanitarian, Philosopher, Artist, Poet, Music Maker, Photographer* and many more including his published articles on *Freedom* and his personal *Letters & Journals*. Here is the life of a man who lived at least twenty lives in the space of one.

FOR FURTHER INFORMATION VISIT
www.lronhubbard.org

GUIDE TO THE MATERIALS

YOU'RE ON AN ADVENTURE!
HERE'S THE MAP.

- All books
- All lectures
- All reference books

All of it laid out in chronological sequence with descriptions of what each contains.

Your journey to a full understanding of Dianetics and Scientology is the greatest adventure of all. But you need a map that shows you where you are and where you are going.

That map is the Materials Guide Chart. It shows all Ron's books and lectures with a full description of their content and subject matter so you can find exactly what *you* are looking for and precisely what *you* need.

Since each book and lecture is laid out in chronological sequence, you can see *how* the subjects of Dianetics and Scientology were developed. And what that means is by simply studying this chart you are in for cognition after cognition!

New editions of all books include extensive glossaries, containing definitions for every technical term. And as a result of a monumental restoration program, the entire library of Ron's lectures are being made available on compact disc, with complete transcripts, glossaries, lecture graphs, diagrams and issues he refers to in the lectures. As a result, you get *all* the data, and can learn with ease, gaining a full *conceptual* understanding.

And what that adds up to is a new Golden Age of Knowledge every Dianeticist and Scientologist has dreamed of.

To obtain your FREE Materials Guide Chart and Catalog, or to order L. Ron Hubbard's books and lectures, contact:

EASTERN HEMISPHERE:
New Era Publications International ApS
Store Kongensgade 53
1264 Copenhagen K, Denmark
www.newerapublications.com
Phone: (45) 33 73 66 66
Fax: (45) 33 73 66 33

WESTERN HEMISPHERE:
Bridge Publications, Inc.
4751 Fountain Avenue
Los Angeles, CA 90029 USA
www.bridgepub.com
Phone: 1-800-722-1733
Fax: 1-323-953-3328

Books and lectures are also available direct from Churches of Scientology.
*See **Addresses**.*

ADDRESSES

Dianetics is a forerunner and substudy of Scientology, the fastest-growing religion in the world today. Centers and Churches exist in cities throughout the world, and new ones are continually forming.

Dianetics Foundations offer introductory services and can help you begin your journey, or get you started on the adventure of Dianetics auditing. To obtain more information or to locate the Dianetics Foundation nearest you, visit the Dianetics website:

www.dianetics.org
e-mail: info@dianetics.org

Every Church of Scientology contains a Dianetics Foundation, offering both introductory services as well as formalized training in the subject. They can also provide further information about Mr. Hubbard's later discoveries on the subject of Scientology. For more information, visit:

www.scientology.org
e-mail: info@scientology.org

You can also write to any one of the Continental Organizations, listed on the following page, who can direct you to one of the thousands of Centers and Churches world over.

L. Ron Hubbard's books and lectures may be obtained from any of these addresses or direct from the publishers on the previous page.

CONTINENTAL ORGANIZATIONS:

EUROPE

CONTINENTAL LIAISON OFFICE EUROPE

Store Kongensgade 55
1264 Copenhagen K, Denmark

Liaison Office of Commonwealth of Independent States
Management Center of Dianetics
and Scientology Dissemination
Pervomajskaya Street, House 1A
Korpus Grazhdanskoy Oboroni
Losino-Petrovsky Town
141150 Moscow, Russia

Liaison Office of Central Europe
1082 Leonardo da Vinci u. 8-14
Budapest, Hungary

Liaison Office of Iberia
C/Miguel Menendez Boneta, 18
28460 – Los Molinos
Madrid, Spain

Liaison Office of Italy
Via Cadorna, 61
20090 Vimodrone
Milan, Italy

AUSTRALIA, NEW ZEALAND & OCEANIA

CONTINENTAL LIAISON OFFICE ANZO

16 Dorahy Street
Dundas, New South Wales 2117
Australia

Liaison Office of Taiwan
1st, No. 231, Cisian 2nd Road
Kaoshiung City
Taiwan, ROC

UNITED STATES

**CONTINENTAL LIAISON OFFICE
WESTERN UNITED STATES**

1308 L. Ron Hubbard Way
Los Angeles, California 90027 USA

**CONTINENTAL LIAISON OFFICE
EASTERN UNITED STATES**

349 W. 48th Street
New York, New York 10036 USA

CANADA

**CONTINENTAL LIAISON OFFICE
CANADA**

696 Yonge Street, 2nd Floor
Toronto, Ontario
Canada M4Y 2A7

LATIN AMERICA

**CONTINENTAL LIAISON OFFICE
LATIN AMERICA**

Federacion Mexicana de Dianetica
Calle Puebla #31
Colonia Roma, Mexico D.F.
C.P. 06700, Mexico

UNITED KINGDOM

**CONTINENTAL LIAISON OFFICE
UNITED KINGDOM**

Saint Hill Manor
East Grinstead, West Sussex
England, RH19 4JY

AFRICA

**CONTINENTAL LIAISON OFFICE
AFRICA**

5 Cynthia Street
Kensington
Johannesburg 2094, South Africa

Become a Member

of the International
Association of Scientologists

The International Association of Scientologists is the membership organization of all Scientologists united in the most vital crusade on Earth.

A free Six-Month Introductory Membership is extended to anyone who has not held a membership with the Association before.

As a member, you are eligible for discounts on Scientology materials offered only to IAS Members. You also receive the Association magazine, *IMPACT,* issued six times a year, full of Scientology news from around the world.

The purpose of the IAS is:

"To unite, advance, support and protect Scientology and Scientologists in all parts of the world so as to achieve the Aims of Scientology as originated by L. Ron Hubbard."

Join the strongest force for positive change on the planet today, opening the lives of millions to the greater truth embodied in Scientology.

Join the International
Association of Scientologists.
To apply for membership,
write to the International
Association of Scientologists
c/o Saint Hill Manor, East Grinstead
West Sussex, England, RH19 4JY

www.iasmembership.org

Editor's Glossary
of Words, Terms & Phrases

Words often have several meanings. The definitions used here only give the meaning that the word has as it is used in this book. Dianetics terms appear in bold type. Beside each definition you will find the page on which it first appears, so you can refer back to the text if you wish.

This glossary is not meant to take the place of standard language or Dianetics and Scientology dictionaries, which should be referred to for any words, terms or phrases that do not appear below.

—The Editors

aberrated: affected by *aberration.* Aberrated conduct would be wrong conduct, or conduct not supported by reason. Aberration is a departure from rational thought or behavior; not sane. *See also* **aberration**. Page 38.

aberration: departure from rational thought or behavior. From the Latin, *aberrare,* to wander from; Latin, *ab,* away, *errare,* to wander. It means basically to err, to make mistakes, or more specifically to have fixed ideas which are not true. The word is also used in its scientific sense. It means departure from a straight line. If a line should go from A to B, then if it is "aberrated" it would go from A to some other point, to some other point, to some other point, to some other point, to some other point and finally arrive at B. Taken in its scientific sense, it would also mean the lack of straightness or to see crookedly as, in example, a man sees a horse but thinks he sees an elephant. Page 13.

aberrative: causing or producing aberration. Page 98.

A-bomb: short for *atomic bomb,* an extremely destructive type of bomb, the power of which results from the immense quantity of energy suddenly released with the splitting of the nuclei (centers) of atoms into several fragments. Page 14.

abreast: side by side; beside each other in a line. Page 191.

absolute: free from restriction or condition; something that is perfect or complete. Page 28.

acute: brief or having a short course as opposed to *chronic* (long-lasting, said of a condition that lasts over a long period). Page 55.

adaptive: of or concerning the process of adjusting oneself to different conditions, environment, etc. Page 189.

adorned: decorated or added beauty to. Page 252.

adroit: skillful in a physical or mental way. Page 112.

ally(ies): **1.** associate or connect by some mutual relationship; befriend. Page 35.
2. an individual who helps or cooperates with another; a supporter or associate; also, a country or group joined with another or others for a common purpose, such as in war, etc. Page 217.

amiable: having or showing pleasant, good-natured personal qualities; friendly. Page 153.

analytical: characterized by awareness, alertness, consciousness, etc. From the Greek *analyze*, resolve, undo, loosen, which is to say, take something to pieces to see what it is made of. Page 91.

anew: once more; again. Page 38.

antipathy: a feeling of disgust toward something usually together with an intense desire to avoid or turn from it. Page 146.

apprehended: taken hold of, seized; arrested. Page 248.

apt: inclined; disposed to; given to; likely. Page 20.

ardent: intensely devoted, eager or enthusiastic. Page 1.

arduous: hard to accomplish; requiring strong effort. Page 296.

armor-plate: insensitive to attack; covered or protected by plating or armor. From the plate or plating of specially hardened steel used to cover warships, tanks, aircraft, fortifications, etc., to protect them from enemy fire. *Armor-plate hide* refers to an armadillo (a burrowing mammal having a protective covering of bony plates) as an example of *"other life forms."* Page 25.

arrested: caught and held; attracted and fixed. Page 221.

arthritis: acute or chronic inflammation of the joints, causing pain, swelling and stiffness. Page 7.

assailed: attacked vigorously or violently. Page 221.

at length: after some time; eventually. Page 200.

attend: take care of; devote one's services to. Page 22.

attendant: accompanying, connected with or immediately following as a consequence. Page 28.

auditing: the application of Dianetics techniques to raise tone and increase perception and memory. Also called *processing*. Page 59.

auditor: a person who administers Dianetics procedures to another; *auditor* means one who listens and computes. Page 5.

avowedly: openly acknowledged or declared. Page 69.

axioms: statements of natural laws on the order of those of the physical sciences. Page 96.

B₁: a B vitamin, found in the outer coating of cereal grains, green peas, beans, egg yolk, liver, etc., and widely available as a vitamin supplement. Page 308.

banister: a handrail (as of a staircase) and its supporting posts. Page 149.

barring: except for. Page 6.

beauty: the combination of qualities that make something pleasing or satisfying to look at as by form, color, texture, line, etc. Also, somebody's girlfriend, wife, etc. In the tale *Beauty and the Beast*, a beautiful and gentle young woman, named Beauty, must befriend a man-beast, Beast, and upon doing so, breaks the evil spell on him whereupon he becomes a handsome prince. Hence, the use of the word *beauty* in *"somebody's beauty."* Page 221.

beholding: holding in view; looking at. Page 215.

bell tolls, for whom the: a reference to a line from the poem "Devotions upon Emergent Occasions" by English poet John Donne (1572-1631), which reads in part: "No man is an island, entire of itself; every man is a piece of the continent, a part of the main...any man's death diminishes me, because I am involved in Mankind; and therefore never send to know for whom the bell tolls; it tolls for thee." Historically, church bells have been tolled (rung slowly) to announce deaths. Page 37.

bent (upon): determined; set; resolved. Page 39.

bested: got the better of; outdid. Page 108.

blind to a fault: from *blind*, unwilling or unable to understand; and *to a fault*, to an extensive degree; excessively. Also, ignore or be unwilling or unable to see a weakness, defect, error, etc. Page 223.

blunted: having the force or keenness weakened or impaired. Page 37.

boil-off: the manifestation of former periods of unconsciousness, accompanied by grogginess. In its English usage, *boil-off* refers to the reduction of quantity of a liquid by its conversion to a gaseous state, such as steam. Boil-off is described in Chapter Ten. Page 105.

bolting: swallowing one's food hurriedly. Page 290.

bootstraps, lifting oneself by one's: raising or bettering oneself by one's own unaided efforts. It alludes to the considerable effort required in pulling on long boots by the means of straps or loops attached to the top of them. Page 65.

box, in a: literally, in a container with a flat bottom and sides and sometimes a lid; in something likened to such a box: a seated compartment in a theater, a sportsman's hiding place while shooting, etc. Figuratively, a colloquial phrase alluding to a difficult position from which there is no escape. Page 224.

breasting: meeting or opposing boldly; confronting. Page 26.

broke bread: broke (tore apart) for one's own mouthfuls. Hence, the phrase means to eat a meal, especially in friendly association with others. Page 224.

bronc: a *bronco,* an untamed or half-tamed horse. Page 7.

brook: a small natural stream of fresh water. Page 183.

burst: to be unable to contain oneself (from expressing or yielding to one's feelings). Hence, *"so happy you felt you would burst."* Page 225.

bursting point: the point at which normal capacity is exceeded. Page 190.

bushel: a unit of dry measure for grain equal to 32 quarts (35.24 liters). Page 20.

cabal: secret intrigue; plot or crafty dealing. Page 71.

caliber: degree of excellence; quality. Page 57.

capricious: tending to change unpredictably or abruptly with no apparent reason; erratic. Page 72.

caravanload: from *caravan,* meaning a group of merchants traveling together using a specific mode of transportation such as pack animals, wagons, etc. Hence, a *caravanload* infers a large quantity. Page 15.

carping: characterized by frequent ill-natured, disgruntled faultfinding. Page 40.

carry home: cause to go to the point aimed at. Hence, execute one's plans successfully. Page 59.

cast: the action of causing to fall upon something or in a certain direction; sending forth. Hence, *"if sometimes clouded over with the not-so-pale cast of bad experience"* infers bad experience throwing a cloud over one's life. Page 5.

catalyze: speed up or, sometimes, slow down the rate of a chemical reaction (as in the body). Page 151.

change one's coat: a coined variation of *turn one's coat,* meaning to change to the opposite party or change sides; to change one's mind or loyalties. Formerly, soldiers wore coats that distinctly showed which army they belonged to. Thus, to turn one's coat was to put one's coat on inside out so as to hide the identifying marks or colors. Page 21.

charged: suffused (gradually spread through or over), as with emotion, such as anger, fear, grief, apathy, etc. Page 97.

charitable: kindly or lenient in judging people, acts, etc. Page 54.

checked: stopped the motion of suddenly or forcibly. Page 290.

chicken broth: in reference to soup made by boiling chicken in water, and traditionally given to sick children by their mothers as a "cure-all." If one can barely stand chicken broth, one cannot handle easy-to-digest food and therefore could not tolerate raw meat unprepared for eating. Used figuratively in *"mental chicken broth."* Page 8.

Christendom: a reference to the whole Western world. Page 3.

chronic: long-lasting, said of an illness or condition that lasts over a long period. Page 53.

chronically: lasting a long time or recurring often. Page 40.

cinch: a sure thing; a certainty. Page 7.

citadels: strongholds. From the fortress commanding a city which is used to control its inhabitants. Page 1.

Clear: an unaberrated person. He is rational in that he forms the best possible solutions he can on the data he has and from his viewpoint. He is called a "Clear" because his basic personality, his self-determinism, his education and experience have been cleared of aberrative engrams, secondaries and locks. See *Dianetics: The Modern Science of Mental Health* and *Science of Survival.* Page 72.

clouded over: that has become gloomy; darkened. Page 5.

coal heaver: a person who carries or shovels coal; a laborer, used in reference to the different strata or professions of society. Page 14.

coat, change one's: a coined variation of *turn one's coat,* meaning to change to the opposite party or change sides; to change one's mind or loyalties. Formerly, soldiers wore coats that distinctly showed which army they belonged to. Thus, to turn one's coat was to put one's coat on inside out so as to hide the identifying marks or colors. Page 21.

co-auditing: auditing by a team of any two people who are auditing each other. Short for *cooperative auditing. See also* **auditing**. Page 59.

coax (something) away: to get something out of someone's possession or use, by gentle means. Page 8.

cocktail: any of various mixed alcoholic drinks. Page 142.

collective state: a state in which people as a group own the land, factories and other means of production, and in exchange all is controlled and paid for by the state (such as medical expenses), as in communism. Page 21.

comm: short for *communication.* Page 71.

committed: placed officially in confinement or custody, especially for a short time. Page 227.

compulsive: having the power to compel; exercising an irresistible impulse to perform an act that is contrary to one's own will. Page 113.

conceded: admitted as true; granted. Page 205.

confounded: 1. defeated utterly, destroyed or overthrown. Page 228.
2. made to feel confused; bewildered. Page 257.

conjurer: one who calls upon or commands spirits or practices magic; a magician. Page 14.

connotation: an additional sense or senses associated with or suggested by a word. Page 193.

constancy: steadfastness of attachment to a person; fidelity. Page 69.

contortionist: a person, as a circus acrobat, who specializes in throwing his body into unnatural or extraordinary positions. Page 187.

contra-survival: from *contra,* against, in opposition to, and *survival.* Hence, *contra-survival* is something in opposition to, against or contrary to survival. Page 215.

control case: a person who is restraining his emotions. As a person is entirely and completely restrained, he's a "good fellow," providing he doesn't show any emotion or quiver. Page 152.

cooled: calmed down or made less excited; lessened the intensity of. Page 291.

coolies: unskilled laborers, used in reference to the different strata or professions of society as in the example, *"You could understand conjurers and bank presidents, colonels and coolies, kings, cats and coal heavers."* Page 14.

criterion: a standard of judgment; a rule or principle for evaluating or testing something. Page 40.

cunning: knowledge of how to do a thing; skill in performance. Page 34.

cut an entrance: to make an opening or passage by cutting through obstructions. Also, to perform or execute an entrance in a showy, striking or impressive way. Page 259.

dash: liveliness and vigor in action or style. Page 59.

deaf ear, turned a: refused to listen to or consider. Page 229.

deaf-mute: a person who is unable to hear and speak, especially one in whom inability to speak is due to early deafness or deafness at birth. Page 199.

defeatist: advocating or accepting defeat; describing a person who surrenders easily or who no longer resists defeat because of the conviction that further effort is futile (incapable of producing any result). Page 47.

dejection: depression or lowness of spirits. Page 151.

delusion: a fixed false belief; a perception that is perceived in a way different from the way it is in reality. From the word *delude,* which means to mislead the mind or judgment of, and *illusion,* which means something that deceives by producing a false or misleading impression of reality. Page 277.

demarcation: the determining and marking off of the boundaries of something, or marking it off from something else. Used figuratively. Page 25.

depository illness: an illness in which deposits of material are formed in some part of the body, such as arthritis where hardened bits of cartilage form in the joints, causing swelling and deformity. Page 68.

depreciate: to fall in value, to become of less worth. Page 193.

dermatitis: inflammation of the skin resulting in redness, swelling, itching or other symptoms. Page 47.

diabetes: a disorder of the body resulting in excessive amounts of sugar in the blood. (It is caused by inadequate production or utilization of *insulin*, a substance produced in one of the glands of the endocrine system.) Page 152.

diabolical: extreme or exceedingly great in degree. Page 14.

Dianetics: from Greek *dia*, through, and *nous*, mind or soul; what the soul is doing to the body. See *Dianetics: The Modern Science of Mental Health* and *Science of Survival*. Page 1.

Dianetic Straightwire: *see* **Straightwire**.

diminish: make smaller or less in scope, quality, etc. Page 38.

diminished: made smaller in size, degree, importance, etc. Page 231.

disabuse: free from error or mistake (as in reasoning or judgment); relieve from deception. Page 8.

disavow: disclaim knowledge of or responsibility for. Page 293.

discordant: not in harmony, clashing. Page 132.

dissipated: dispersed (from a more concentrated form); alleviated; made (something) vanish. Page 273.

dissipating: diminishing; fading or vanishing. Page 104.

dived in: entered deeply or plunged into a subject, activity, etc. Page 231.

dope: any narcotic or narcotic-like drug taken to induce euphoria or satisfy addiction. Page 22.

down to size, pull: a variation of *cut down to size*, meaning to reduce the prestige or importance of someone; to show someone that he is not as important or as good as he thinks he is. Page 293.

dregs: the last remaining parts (often, the least valuable). Page 190.

drives: inner urges that stimulate activity; energy and initiative. Page 14.

dynamic: active, energetic, effective, forceful, motivating, as opposed to static. From the Greek *dunamikos*, powerful. Page 19.

dynamics: the dynamics are the urge to survive expressed through a spectrum with eight divisions. These are urges for survival as or through (1) self; (2) sex, the family and the future generation; (3) groups; (4) Mankind; (5) life, all organisms; (6) matter, energy, space and time—MEST—the physical universe; (7) spirits; and (8) the Supreme Being. The subject of the dynamics is contained in *Science of Survival*. Page 72.

ear, turned a deaf: refused to listen to or consider. Page 229.

easy chair: a stuffed or padded armchair for lounging. Page 147.

effect: 1. something caused or produced; a result. Page 7.
2. bring about; accomplish; make happen. Page 191.

electrons: negatively charged particles that form a part of all atoms. Page 33.

endocrine: of or having to do with the system of glands which secretes hormones (chemical substances) from certain organs and tissues in the body. These glands and their hormones regulate the growth, development and function of certain tissues and coordinate many processes within the body. For example, some of these glands increase blood pressure and heart rate during times of stress. Page 68.

engrams: recordings of moments of pain and unconsciousness. These recordings can be later brought into play by a similar word or environment and cause the individual to act as though in the presence of danger. They force the individual into patterns of thinking and behavior which are not called for by a reasonable appraisal of the situation. A description of engrams and their relevance to *Self Analysis* is contained in Chapter Ten, Processing Section. The complete description of engrams is contained in *Dianetics: The Modern Science of Mental Health* and *Science of Survival*. Page 9.

enmity: the feelings characteristic of an enemy; ill will, hatred, especially when mutual. Page 242.

entheta: a compound word meaning *enturbulated theta,* theta in a turbulent state, agitated or disturbed. *See also* **theta**. Page 71.

entheta lines: entheta communication lines, lines which are vicious or slanderous. Page 71.

entrance, cut an: to make an opening or passage by cutting through obstructions. Also, to perform or execute an entrance in a showy, striking or impressive way. Page 259.

entranced: filled with delight; charmed with. Page 232.

enturbulates: causes turbulence, agitation and disturbance. Page 69.

enturbulences: things which are in a turbulent, agitated or disturbed state; commotions and upsets. Page 40.

environ: environment; surroundings. Page 69.

esoteric: beyond the understanding or knowledge of most people. Page 22.

ESP: extrasensory perception, perception or communication outside of normal sensory capability, as in telepathy. Page 98.

ethics: rationality toward the highest level of survival for self and others. Page 61.

euthanasia: also called "mercy killing," the act of putting to death painlessly or allowing to die, as by withholding extreme medical measures, a person or animal suffering from an incurable, especially a painful, disease or condition. Page 39.

evaluate: work out or measure the value of. Page 71.

faces, made: made a face; contorted one's face to convey a feeling or amuse oneself or another. (*Contort* means to distort one's features by tensing or contracting the facial muscles.) Page 282.

fad: a temporary fashion, notion, manner of conduct, etc., especially one followed enthusiastically by a group. Page 3.

fainthearted: lacking energy, courage or will to carry a thing through. Page 9.

fascist: one who practices *fascism*, a governmental system led by a dictator having complete power, which forcibly suppresses opposition and criticism and regiments all industry, commerce, etc. Page 39.

fault, blind to a: from *blind*, unwilling or unable to understand; and *to a fault*, to an extensive degree; excessively. Also, ignore or be unwilling or unable to see a weakness, defect, error, etc. Page 223.

feet, landed on one's: literally, came down to a surface on one's feet, as a cat does when falling from a height. Figuratively, ended up healthy or in a good position, especially after having been sick or in a difficult situation. Page 236.

fillet: a boneless cut or slice of meat; a beefsteak. Page 142.

flare: flare up; light up, go into a sudden outburst or intensification, as of anger or tensions. Page 8.

flick through: from the word *flicker*, a television and film term referring to sudden abrupt changes of picture when the number of frames per second is too small to produce one continuous image. Hence, "*many unhappy incidents will flick through*" refers to random images of those incidents coming to view when remembering what is asked for in the processing question. Page 200.

flighty: given to sudden whims (sudden or odd desires); not taking things seriously; frivolous (lack of seriousness) or irresponsible. Page 72.

foolhardy: bold or daring in a foolish way; reckless. Page 46.

fortitude: mental and emotional strength in facing difficulty, adversity or danger courageously. Page 293.

for want of: for lack of; because of the absence or deficiency of. Page 290.

for whom the bell tolls: a reference to a line from the poem "Devotions upon Emergent Occasions" by English poet John Donne (1572-1631), which reads in part: "No man is an island, entire of itself; every man is a piece of the continent, a part of the main...any man's death diminishes me, because I am involved in Mankind; and therefore never send to know for whom the bell tolls; it tolls for thee." Historically, church bells have been tolled (rung slowly) to announce deaths. Page 37.

function: intellectual powers; mental action; thought. Page 152.

gaiety: the state of being joyous and lively, merry or cheerful; gay spirits. Page 73.

gala: characterized by display of show, festivity, joy and merrymaking. Page 239.

gate, gave somebody the: dismissed somebody from one's employ; rejected somebody. Page 161.

gentleman with the scythe: a reference to the *Grim Reaper*, a representation of Death, often portrayed as a man or cloaked skeleton carrying and using a scythe in his duty as a "harvester" or "collector" of bodies and souls. (A *scythe* is an agricultural instrument with a curved cutting blade attached to a sticklike handle, used for cutting grass, grain, etc.) Page 28.

graces, social: procedures or attitudes producing favorable impressions, attractiveness or charm. Page 73.

graduated scale: a scale of condition graduated from zero to infinity. The word *graduated* is meant to define lessening or increasing degrees of condition. The difference between one point on a graduated scale and another point could be as different or as wide as the entire range of the scale itself, or it could be so tiny as to need the most minute discernment (ability to perceive the difference) for its establishment. Page 22.

graybeards: men with gray beards; hence, old men. Page 26.

grounded: stuck, as of a ship, boat, etc.; run ashore or aground. Page 9.

Group Dianetic: having to do with *Group Dianetics*, that branch of Dianetics which embraces the field of group activity and organization to establish the optimum (best or most favorable) conditions and processes of leadership and intergroup relations. Page 5.

guidon: a small flag, broad at one end and pointed or forked at the other end, originally carried by the military for identification. Used figuratively. Page 1.

haggard: having a wasted or exhausted appearance from prolonged suffering or anxiety. Page 21.

hand, at every: in all directions; everywhere; on all sides. *Hand* is used here to mean direction or side and is a reference to the position of the hands—one on either side of the body. Page 122.

hand, on every: a variation of *at every turn*, meaning constantly, on every occasion or in every case. Page 13.

harken: give heed or attention to what is said; listen. Page 3.

harnessed: brought under conditions for effective use; gained control over for a particular end. Page 111.

hasten: speed up, accelerate. Page 39.

hastened: moved or acted with speed; hurried. Page 234.

hearsay evidence: testimony based on what a witness has heard from another person rather than on direct personal knowledge or experience. Page 98.

hitherto: up to this time; until now. Page 41.

hole, in the: inside of a hollow place or cavity within a solid body. *Hole* has various meanings such as an opening in the ground, a dungeon or prison cell, etc. Figuratively, in an embarrassing position or predicament; in difficult circumstances. Page 235.

homelier: more homely, that is, lacking in physical attractiveness; not beautiful; unattractive. Page 296.

hooky, played: stayed away from school without permission. Page 211.

hunted: chased, pursued or searched for (persons, wild animals, etc.) with the purpose of finding, catching, killing and so forth. Page 235.

hypothyroid: of or relating to a physical disorder resulting from deficient activity of the thyroid gland. The thyroid secretes chemical substances that regulate body growth and metabolism. *Hypo* means "under" as opposed to *hyper* which means "excess" or "exaggerated." Page 152.

ignominiously: in a humiliating or degrading manner. Page 59.

illuminated: 1. brightened with light. Page 168.
2. enlightened, as with knowledge. Page 235.

illustrate: shed light upon; make clear; explain (such as by examples, comparisons, etc.). Page 286.

illustrative: serving to illustrate; explanatory. Page 57.

implanted: fixed something deeply in somebody's mind as a behavior pattern, thought or belief. Page 191.

incident: an individual occurrence or event. Page 89.

income tax blank: income tax form, a blank form sent to taxpayers on which one accounts for and calculates the amount of tax due to the government. Page 8.

in vain: without effect or purpose; to no avail. Page 172.

jack rabbit: any of various large hares of western North America, having very long hind legs and long ears. Wolves typically hunt jack rabbits, so a jack rabbit spitting in a wolf's eyes would be extremely bold or daring. *"It'd make a jack rabbit spit in a wolf's eye"* is used figuratively to mean that it would make one overcome one's fears so as to boldly stare down or back off one's enemies. Page 7.

"Know thyself!": one of the essential principles in the philosophy of Greek philosopher Socrates (470–399 B.C.). Page 13.

knuckle under: submit to; yield. Page 61.

Lake Tanganyika: the longest freshwater lake in the world, located in east central Africa. Page 191.

landed on one's feet: literally, came down to a surface on one's feet, as a cat does when falling from a height. Figuratively, ended up healthy or in a good position, especially after having been sick or in a difficult situation. Page 236.

laughed last: were proved right or successful after being treated with disbelief, lack of confidence or strong criticism; turned out to be successful in the end (after a seeming defeat or loss). *Laugh* here is used in connection with the celebration of victory, sometimes by making fun of someone or something after winning a contest or something thought of as a contest. Page 168.

lest: for fear that. Page 216.

lick: overcome or defeat. Page 7.

lion's share: the largest part or share, especially a disproportionate portion. Page 297.

lock(s): a moment of mental discomfort containing no physical pain and no great loss. A scolding, a social disgrace; such things are locks. Any case has thousands and thousands of locks. Page 96.

look (someone or something) in the eye: look directly at; confront in a way that shows courage, confidence or (sometimes) defiance. Page 27.

lot: one's fate, fortune or destiny. Page 21.

Man: the human race or species, humankind, Mankind. Page 1.

man: a human being, without regard to sex or age; a person. Page 3.

mania: excessive excitement or enthusiasm, madness. Page 289.

manifestation: the demonstration or display of the qualities or nature of some person; a perceptible, outward or visible expression. Page 57.

marts: meeting places for the buying and selling of goods; trading centers or markets. Page 13.

materially: to a great extent; substantially. Page 308.

mayhap: perhaps. Page 26.

minded: took care of; looked after. Page 238.

minions of the Devil: a minion is a servile (slavelike) follower or subordinate of a person in power. The phrase comes from the religious concept (Christianity and other faiths) that those opposed to God fight for the Devil and in the name of evil. Hence, "*minions of the Devil.*" Page 22.

misapprehension: the action of failing to understand correctly, or taking the wrong meaning of. Page 182.

misconstrued: misunderstood as to the meaning; taken in the wrong sense. Page 206.

mis-emotional: exhibiting or displaying mis-emotion. *Mis-* means mistaken, wrong, incorrect; thus *mis*-emotion is any emotion that is irrational or inappropriate to the present time environment. Page 151.

monocell: an organism composed of a single cell. Page 33.

---

negation: a refusal or contradiction; a denial of something. Page 54.

neurological: having to do with the nerves and the nervous system. Page 68.

New Yorker: an American weekly magazine founded in 1925 which specializes in satire, social commentary and criticism. Page 59.

Niagara: an overwhelming flood of something, taken as resembling Niagara Falls in volume, force and relentlessness. (Niagara Falls is a large waterfall located at the border between America and Canada.) Page 192.

occasioned: brought about; caused. Page 124.

occluded: having memories shut off from one's awareness; from *occlude,* to close, shut or stop up (a passage, opening, etc.). Page 99.

old man: a familiar term for one's father or husband. It can also refer to a person in a position of authority as one's boss, a military superior, etc. Page 297.

olfactory: of or pertaining to the sense of smell. Page 138.

optimum: most favorable or desirable; best. Page 37.

out of sight: used in reference to discoveries, information or the like that, while not specifically listed, are still present. Literally, not visible; outside or beyond the range or field of vision. Page 103.

outward bound: departing this life, dying, or preparing, starting or going in the direction of death. From the nautical use meaning headed in an outward direction, as toward foreign ports; going away from home. Hence, *"outward bound toward death."* Page 38.

palatable: acceptable or agreeable to the mind or feelings. Page 9.

pale: not bright or brilliant; dim. Page 5.

pancreas: a gland situated behind the stomach that secretes digestive juice into the small intestine. Page 152.

pennyweights: units of weight equal to ¹⁄₂₀th of an ounce or 1.6 grams. The pennyweight was once the weight of a silver penny. Page 48.

perceptics: perceived and recorded sense messages, such as smell, taste, touch, sound, sight, etc.; perceptions. Page 100.

persevering: persisting in an undertaking in spite of difficulty, obstacles or discouragement. Page 104.

Persian: of or pertaining to Persia, an ancient empire located in western and southwestern Asia that included parts of what is now Iran. Page 14.

perversion: 1. any of various means of obtaining sexual gratification that are generally regarded as abnormal. Page 69.
2. a turning aside from truth or right; diversion to an improper use. Page 70.

physiology: the functions and activities of living organisms and their parts, including all physical and chemical processes. Page 56.

played hooky: stayed away from school without permission. Page 211.

plutonium: a radioactive metallic element that is used in nuclear reactors and nuclear weapons. Page 48.

poker: a metal rod for poking or stirring a fire. Page 147.

posed: offered (as a threat). Page 54.

poses: **1.** puts forth for examination; questions. Page 36.
2. assumes a certain attitude. Page 58.

positive suggestion: in hypnosis, a suggestion or command which is given to a hypnotized subject who then obeys it unwittingly. Page 73.

postulate(s): **1.** assume (something) to be true, real or necessary, especially as a basis for reasoning. Page 15.
2. something that is suggested or assumed to be true as a basis for reasoning. Page 96.
3. to put something forth (so as to exist); create. Page 277.

preclear: an individual entering upon and undergoing Dianetic Processing who is not yet a Clear. Page 95.

processes: exact series of directions or sequences of actions that, when applied, help a person find out more about himself and his life and improve his condition. Page 8.

processing: the application of Dianetics techniques and exercises. Also called *auditing*. Page 7.

prodigiously: in a large amount, extent, degree, quantity, etc. Page 173.

promiscuity: the condition or state of being *promiscuous*, having sexual relations with a number of partners on a casual basis. Page 69.

pro-survival: from *pro*, in favor of, and *survival*. Hence, *pro-survival* describes something in favor of or in support of survival. Page 215.

protons: the positively charged particles that form a part of all atoms. Page 33.

prudent: careful in providing for the future. Page 20.

psychosomatic: *psycho* refers to mind and *somatic* refers to body; the term *psychosomatic* means the mind making the body ill or illnesses which have been created physically within the body by the mind. The description of the cause and source of psychosomatic ills is contained in *Dianetics: The Modern Science of Mental Health*. Page 7.

pungent: sharply affecting the organs of taste or smell, as if by a penetrating power; biting. Page 138.

punishment-drive: the psychological practice of inflicting pain, deprivation (the action of removing or withholding something from the enjoyment or possession of someone) or other unpleasant consequences on an individual to make him or her avoid what is considered by the practitioner undesirable action or behavior. Page 190.

qualms: uneasy feelings of doubt or conscience about an action or conduct. Page 260.

quarter, cried for: a military term used figuratively; called for mercy to be shown in sparing the life of one who surrenders. Page 297.

raw meat: uncooked meat. *See also* **chicken broth**. Page 8.

realize: make real; give reality to. Page 37.

recaptured: recollected or re-experienced from the past. Page 102.

recrimination: the action of bringing a counter-accusation against a person. Page 293.

reevaluate: evaluate again; analyze a second or further time. *See also* **evaluate**. Page 218.

regimentation: state of being regimented. *See also* **regimented**. Page 21.

regimented: organized in a rigid system under strict discipline and control. Page 26.

rejoice: be glad or take delight in; be full of joy. Page 149.

relishes: takes pleasure in; likes; enjoys. Page 57.

repulsion: the action of forcing or driving back or away. Page 59.

restimulated: reactivated; stimulated (again). Page 105.

resurgences: acts of rising again or springing again into being or vigor. Page 39.

revelry: boisterous (noisy and jolly) merrymaking; festivity. Page 136.

rheumatism: disorder of the extremities (limbs, hands or feet) or back, characterized by pain and stiffness. Page 47.

rims: edges or borders. Page 58.

root stuff: the basic cause, source or origin of some quality or condition. *Stuff* in this sense means the fundamental material of which something is made or consists; essence. Page 8.

ruler: a strip of wood, metal or other material having a straight edge for use in drawing straight lines. Page 80.

run out: in Dianetics, *run out* means to exhaust the negative influence of something; to erase. Page 95.

Russell, Charles (Charlie): (1864-1926) painter of the American West who used his experiences as a trapper and cowboy to provide material for paintings of the "Old West" (cowboys, etc.). Page 7.

sages: wise men; persons of profound wisdom. Page 14.

satiated: satisfied, as one's appetite or desire, to the point of boredom. Page 155.

savant: a person of extensive learning. Page 9.

scythe, gentleman with the: a reference to the *Grim Reaper,* a representation of Death, often portrayed as a man or cloaked skeleton carrying and using a scythe in his duty as a "harvester" or "collector" of bodies and souls. (A *scythe* is an agricultural instrument with a curved cutting blade attached to a sticklike handle, used for cutting grass, grain, etc.) Page 28.

secondaries: moments of acute loss, as death of a loved one, called secondaries as they depend upon an earlier engram for their force on the individual. The subject of secondaries and their processing is contained in *Science of Survival.* Page 95.

seed (wheat): reserved for planting to grow the next crop. Page 20.

seized: grasped suddenly or forcibly. Page 247.

self-determinism: that state of being wherein the individual can or cannot be controlled by his environment according to his own choice. In that state the individual has self-confidence in his control of the material universe and the organisms within it. He is confident about any and all abilities or talents he may possess. He is confident in his interpersonal relationships. He reasons but does not need to react. Page 27.

session: a period of time given to or set aside for the pursuit of a particular activity. In Dianetics, it refers to a period of time set aside for processing, the application of Dianetics techniques and exercises. Page 95.

shadow personality: the taking on of the physical and/or emotional characteristics or traits of another. Page 281.

shoal: a place where a sea, river or other body of water is shallow. Page 191.

shooting star: a meteor, resembling a star, that darts across the sky. Page 184.

shut the door on: prevented the possibility of or access to (an opening). Page 239.

sinews: strong fibrous cords serving to connect muscles with bones or other parts; tendons. Page 28.

singing: giving out a continuous ringing, whistling, murmuring or other sound of a musical character. Page 134.

sketch over: review in general. Page 309.

slipshod: marked by indifference or carelessness. Page 72.

slurred: said or spoken of, so as to injure the credit or reputation of. Page 296.

social graces: procedures or attitudes producing favorable impressions, attractiveness or charm. Page 73.

socialism: an economic system in which the production and distribution of goods are controlled by the government rather than by individuals. Page 21.

sonic: the recall of something heard, so that it is heard again in the mind in full tone and strength. Page 133.

sore at: angry, annoyed or offended toward someone. Page 245.

spinning: going into a state of mental confusion. Page 8.

sporadic: appearing in scattered or isolated instances. Page 68.

squandered: spent or used money extravagantly or wastefully. Page 269.

standard: a flag or other object raised on a pole to indicate the rallying point of an army, fleet, etc. Page 1.

starting: giving a sudden, involuntary jerk, jump or twitch, as from a shock of surprise, alarm or pain. Page 132.

statically: in a fixed or stationary way. Page 217.

stereophonic: noting or pertaining to three-dimensional sound by the use of two channels of reproduction (such as speakers) so that the sound may seem to reach the listener from any range of directions, giving the impression of spacial dimension. *Stereophonic* literally means lifelike sound, as *stereo* means solid and *phonic* means sound. Page 133.

stereoscopic: noting or pertaining to three-dimensional vision—the dimensions of height, width and depth. From the word *stereoscope*, an optical instrument through which two pictures of the same object, taken from slightly different points of view, are viewed, one by each eye, producing the effect of a single picture of the object with the appearance of depth; hence, three-dimensional. *Stereoscopic* literally means lifelike vision, as *stereo* means solid and *scopic* means to look at. Page 124.

stick (to the finish): to keep to a task or undertaking to completion. Page 233.

stirred: caused to be emotionally moved or strongly affected; excited. Page 246.

stopped over: briefly interrupted one's course of movement, travel, etc., for a brief stay, such as to visit or see somebody. Page 246.

straightedge: a strip of wood, plastic or metal having a straight edge for use in drawing straight lines. Page 80.

Straightwire: a process that puts one into better communication with his mind and the world. It is so called because the preclear is being directed, much like a telephone wire, directly to a memory in the past. Communication is opened between the past and the present. The person undergoing processing is in present time and in contact with present time and he is asked questions which restore to him certain memories. Page 65.

striking up: beginning or causing to begin a friendship, acquaintance or the like, often in a casual way; bringing into being. Page 13.

stripped: deprived someone of what was his. Page 246.

subjugate: bring under complete control. Page 190.

sublimated: turned into something higher, nobler or more refined. Page 69.

subversive: one who seeks to overthrow or destroy an established or legally constructed government, institution, etc. Page 21.

suspect: regarded with suspicion or distrust. Page 47.

suspected: believed to be the case or to be likely or probable. Page 13.

sustenance: means of sustaining life; nourishment. Page 68.

swanky: elegant, expensive and showy. Page 144.

tenets: principles, doctrines. Page 48.

theta: the energy of thought and life. *Theta* is reason, serenity, stability, happiness, cheerful emotion, persistence and the other factors which Man ordinarily considers desirable. The complete description of theta is contained in *Science of Survival*. Page 71.

throw a wheel: a coined phrase meaning to cease making good progress; to stop running or operating smoothly. To *throw* means to break or render inoperable and *wheel* alludes to the wheel of a vehicle, such as a wagon. From the days of horse-drawn wagons and carriages: when traveling over rough terrain, the wheels tended to break off, thus stopping the wagon and any further travel until repaired. Page 8.

thyroid: a reference to the thyroid gland, which secretes hormones (chemical substances) that regulate body growth and metabolism. Page 152.

tide: a body of flowing water; a current. Used figuratively here in the *"tide of life"* to mean the moving force of life. Page 39.

tone: one's emotional level. Page 7.

tooth and claw: a variation of *tooth and nail,* with the use of one's teeth and nails as weapons, by biting and scratching. Used figuratively in the way of vigorous attack, defense or action generally; vigorously, fiercely, with one's utmost efforts, with all one's might. Page 132.

tractability: the condition of being tractable; easily managed or controlled; docile; yielding. Page 190.

trance: 1. to put in a trance or hypnotic condition. Page 73.
2. also called *hypnotic trance,* a state, as induced by hypnosis, in which somebody is dazed or stunned or in some other way not fully aware of the present environment. Page 73.

tribute: a gift, testimonial, compliment or the like, given as due or in acknowledgment of gratitude or esteem. Page 268.

truant officer: an official who investigates unauthorized absences from school. Page 8.

truism: a self-evident, obvious truth. Page 26.

trying: extremely annoying, difficult or the like; straining one's patience and goodwill to the limit. Page 128.

tug of war: an athletic contest between two teams holding on to and pulling at opposite ends of a rope, each team trying to drag the other over a line in the middle. Page 177.

twilight: a terminal (occurring at or causing the end of life) period, especially after full development, as in "the twilight of his life." Page 58.

unavailing: being of no use. Page 55.

universe: everything that exists everywhere; the whole space-time continuum in which we exist, together with all the energy and matter within it, as opposed to, and greater than, the observable universe. Page 19.

vacillation: the act of wavering in mind, will or feeling; hesitation in choice of opinions or courses. Page 72.

vain: excessively proud of or concerned about one's own appearance, qualities, achievements, etc. Page 165.

vain, in: without effect or purpose; to no avail. Page 172.

valences: literally, the word means the ability to combine with or take on parts of another. In Dianetics, *valence* is an actual or shadow personality. One's own valence is his actual personality. *See also* **shadow personality**. Page 281.

Validation: refers to Validation Technique of processing whereby the concentration is on the analytical moments of any given incident, as opposed to the painful moments. A full description of Validation Technique is contained in *Science of Survival*. Page 65.

Validation MEST Processing: processing whereby the concentration is on the analytical moments of any given incident, as opposed to the painful moments. This processing also orients the individual to the present time and the physical universe—matter, energy, space and time—MEST. A full description of this type of processing is contained in *Science of Survival*. Page 65.

virtuous: conforming to moral and ethical principles and virtues (the ideal qualities in good human conduct). Page 160.

vital: full of vigor; energetic. Page 27.

vitality: enthusiastic physical strength or mental vigor. Page 26.

volatile: apt to change; liable to display rapid changes of emotion. Page 69.

voodoo: a body of beliefs and practices originally from Africa that includes magic and the supposed exercise of supernatural powers through the aid of evil spirits. Page 48.

warranted: justified (by the circumstances); serving as reasonable grounds for (an act, belief, etc.). Page 132.

Washington: George Washington (1732-1799), first president of the United States (1789-1797). Washington's face appears in the center of the dollar bill. Page 6.

welfare state: a state in which the welfare of the people in such matters as social security, health and education, housing and working conditions is the responsibility of the government. Page 190.

wheedle: try to influence or persuade by smooth, flattering words. Page 22.

whence: from where? from what place, source, cause, etc.? Page 14.

wherewithal: that with which to do something; means or supplies for the purpose or need. Page 21.

whipped: defeated or overcome. Page 27.

whirl: turn around, spin or rotate rapidly. Page 7.

whither: to what place? where? to what end, point, action or the like? to what? Page 14.

won out: won or succeeded, especially over great odds; triumphed. Page 197.

Word, the: a reference to a quote from the Bible: "In the beginning was the Word." The "Word" here refers to the word of God. Page 14.

wrested: gained with difficulty by or as if by force, violent action or steady determined labor. Page 264.

wrong: something not in accordance with morality, goodness or truth; evil. Page 212.

zest: liveliness or energy. Page 28.

INDEX

C

cabal, 71

capabilities
  become a great deal more, 14

cases
  opening, 95

cells
  life and, 34
  organism and loss of, 46
  pain and loss of, 206
  see also **monocell**

characteristics
  constant across Chart of Human
    Evaluation boxes, 54

charge
  removal from painful
    incidents, 97

Chart of Human Evaluation, 65-75
  at the top of, 57
  constant characteristics across
    boxes, 54
  decline on, 57
  Self Analysis and, 60
  self-evaluation, 7
  test to place self on, 8, 60, 61
  see also **Tone Scale**

chicken broth, 8

child (children)
  attitude toward, 69
  childhood incident, 128
  forced loss of objects and, 205
  going down the scale,
    example, 206
  interrupted in his physical
    actions, 287
  punishment and training of, 206
  slapping of, 182
  suppressed by parents and
    school, 40
  surrounded with large
    objects, 128
  survival potentialities, 217
  threatened by danger, 54
  Tone Scale and examples, 54
  wants a nickel, 58
  words and, 97, 192, 199

chronic position (Chart of Human
  Evaluation), 65

chronic somatics, 91

Clear, 72

clearing
  of engrams and secondaries, 96

co-auditing, 95
  Dianetics, 59

cold or heat, 145

collective state, 26

color perception, 101, 124
  colorblindness, 124

communication
  Recall a time when someone was
    in good communication with
    you, 307
  senses and channels of, 145
  sound and, 98
  Tone Scale, 71

computer
memory accurate as, 6

concept
recalls, if only vague, 90
recovering actual perception
of, 99

consciousness
death of, 25-29
decline of, 25, 28, 57
full, definition, 40
lessening of, 46
not an absolute thing, 28
raising of, 45-49
return to full, 46
what it depends upon, 47

conservative
chronic, 58
3.0 on Tone Scale, 54
see also **Chart of Human
Evaluation**

control
hidden, 73
over environment, 25
two aberrated methods, 293
with force, 38

control case
definition, 152

conversation, 71

courage, 70

covert hostility, 151
see also **Chart of Human
Evaluation**

coward, 70
method of domination, 293

criminal
survival of, 22

criticism
of others for "their own good," 40

cycle
of conception, birth, growth,
decay and death, 35

D

danger
child threatened by, 54
environment and, 182
motion, safe or, 182

daydreaming, 277

deafness
deaf-mute, 199
definition, 133
psychosomatic and, 133

death
beginnings of, 39
body and, 35
cycle of conception, birth,
growth, decay and, 35
definition, 28
description, 38
half unconsciousness, half
death, 28
life has a use for, 38
of consciousness, 25-29
of organism, 26
of reason, 26
on a small scale, 40
pain and
warning of potential, 35
warning of source of, 46

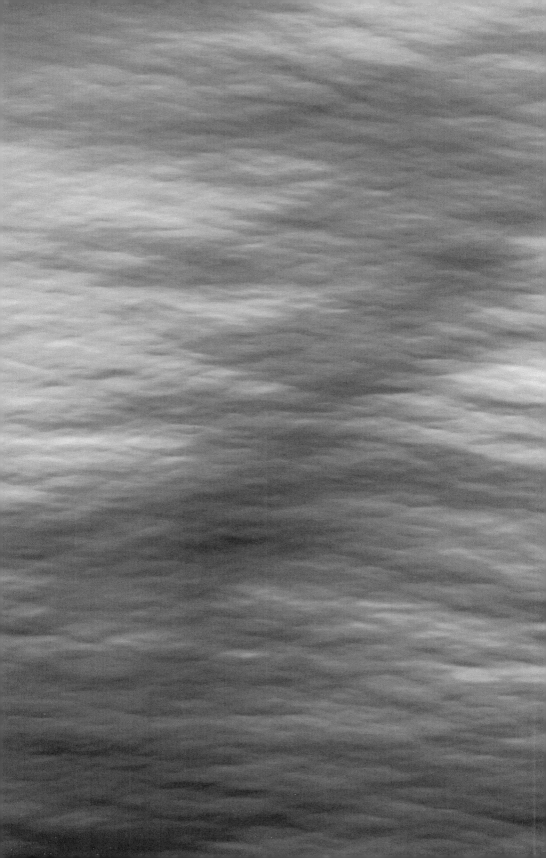